RETIREMENT REDEFINED FOR WOMEN

NAVIGATE LIFE AFTER WORK WITH CONFIDENCE, BUILD COMMUNITY, EXPLORE PASSIONS, AND STAY ENGAGED TO LIVE YOUR BEST LIFE

VICTORIA SPRING

CONTENTS

INTRODUCTION

As I sat across from my dear friend Sarah, watching her eyes brim with tears, I couldn't help but feel a deep sense of empathy. "I thought retirement would be a time of freedom and joy," she confessed, "but instead, I feel lost and alone." Her words echoed the sentiments of countless women I've encountered over the years, each grappling with the profound changes that come with leaving their careers behind.

The unique challenges women face as they transition into retirement have been overlooked for far too long. We're expected to embrace this new chapter gracefully, yet few resources exist to guide us through the complex emotional, social, and financial landscape that lies ahead. It's time to change that narrative.

This book was born from a desire to empower women like Sarah – and like you – to redefine retirement on your own terms. As someone who has walked this path myself, I understand the fears, doubts, and aspirations that come with this significant life shift. My goal is to provide a roadmap that addresses the practical aspects of retirement planning and delves into the deeper questions of identity, purpose, and fulfillment.

Throughout these pages, we'll explore the holistic dimensions of retirement, from building a solid financial foundation to nurturing meaningful relationships and discovering new passions. You'll find real-life stories from women who have successfully navigated this journey, as well as practical exercises and reflections designed to help you clarify your vision for the future.

But this book is more than a guide; it's an invitation to undertake a transformative journey of self-discovery. As you read, I encourage you to approach each chapter with an open mind and willingness to challenge long-held beliefs about what retirement "should" look like. This is your opportunity to create a life that truly resonates with your values, desires, and dreams.

Together, we'll delve into the art of crafting a retirement that is uniquely yours. We'll explore how to cultivate resilience in the face of change, build a supportive network of like-minded women, and prioritize self-care as you adjust to your new normal. You'll learn strategies for staying mentally sharp, physically active, and emotionally grounded, ensuring your retirement years are filled with vitality and purpose.

As we move through each chapter, you'll gain clarity, confidence, and a renewed sense of excitement for the possibilities that lie ahead. Whether you're on the cusp of retirement or have already taken the leap, this book will serve as a trusted companion, offering guidance, inspiration, and a reminder that you are not alone on this journey.

So, dear reader, I invite you to turn the page and join me on this transformative adventure. Together, we'll redefine retirement and unlock the secrets to crafting a joyful, engaged lifestyle that honors your unique gifts and aspirations. Let's embark on this journey with open hearts and minds, ready to embrace the incredible opportunities that await us in this new chapter of life.

1

REDEFINING YOUR IDENTITY BEYOND THE CAREER

At a recent gathering, I met Diane, a woman who, after decades of dedication to her career, stood at the precipice of retirement. "I spent my life defining myself by my work," she shared, "and now, I wonder who I am without my job title." Her words resonate with many women who face similar crossroads. This chapter invites you to explore the exciting opportunity that retirement offers to redefine your identity, not as a loss but as a chance to focus on personal growth, new interests, and uncharted paths. This transition isn't just about retiring from work; it's about rediscovering yourself and embracing a phase rich with potential.

1.1 EMBRACING THE NEW YOU: A PERSONAL JOURNEY

The transition from a career-driven life to one centered on personal identity can feel daunting, yet it holds the promise of transformation. Instead of viewing retirement as an end, see it as a beginning—a time to shift focus from professional roles to personal growth. Reflecting on past achievements and future aspirations can provide clarity. Consider dedicating time to exercises that help you recognize the skills and strengths you've developed over the years. Write them down, celebrate them, and then envision how these can be applied to new pursuits. Reflect on what you've always wanted to explore but never had the time for. This is the moment to let those dreams flourish. To illustrate this, let's look at Catherine Kilty, a nonprofit director who transitioned to a post-retirement life filled with alternative income sources that aligned with her passions. Catherine's story exemplifies how embracing change can lead to a fulfilling and purpose-driven life.

As you embark on this personal journey, it's crucial to foster self-acceptance and growth. This involves acknowledging the emotional aspects of redefining yourself and overcoming the fear of change. Many women find it challenging to move beyond the roles they've held for so long, but developing a growth mindset can ease this transition. Techniques such as cognitive reframing can be invaluable, where you consciously shift negative thoughts to positive ones. Embrace the idea that retirement is a time for reinvention, not regression. By gradually letting go of past job titles and the identity tied to them, you can open the door to new opportunities. Writing a farewell letter to your career can serve as a powerful ritual for closure. Express gratitude for experiences and lessons learned, then consciously release them, making space for the future.

Creating a vision for what lies ahead is a pivotal step in this process. Picture a future where you are free to explore new interests without the constraints of a work schedule. Consider attending a vision board workshop where you can visually map out goals and aspirations. This creative exercise allows you to focus on what truly matters to you and serves as a tangible reminder of your intentions. Goal-setting exercises can also help you chart a course for personal development. Break down your aspirations into steps and set realistic timelines to keep yourself accountable. As you progress, celebrate each milestone, no matter how small, to maintain momentum and motivation.

Reflection Exercise: Mapping Your Past and Future

Take a moment to reflect on your career and personal life. Write down three significant achievements you're proud of and consider how they have shaped you. Then, list three aspirations you have for the future. Reflect on how these aspirations align with your values and passions. How can you begin to integrate these into your daily life? This exercise bridges who you've been and who you're becoming, helping you embrace the new you with confidence.

The journey to redefine your identity beyond your career is as unique as you are. It requires courage and a willingness to embrace change. You can navigate this transition with enthusiasm by focusing on personal growth, recognizing your strengths, and setting new goals. Retirement is not just a phase of life; it's a canvas upon which you can paint a vibrant and fulfilling future. As you continue through this book, let these insights inspire you to explore all this new chapter offers.

1.2 FROM JOB TITLE TO PERSONAL FULFILLMENT

During retirement, a profound shift occurs as we transition our focus from professional achievements to personal satisfaction. This change invites us to redefine fulfillment, moving away from the metrics of job titles and salary increases and toward the more enriching realm of personal values and happiness. Identifying what truly matters to us becomes a guiding compass in this transition. Take a moment to reflect on your core values—those deep-seated beliefs that have shaped your life decisions. Aligning these values with new activities can create a more satisfying and meaningful existence. Whether it's nurturing creativity through painting or fostering connections by volunteering, these pursuits can bring a sense of accomplishment that transcends any corporate accolade.

Finding fulfillment in new roles often means stepping into spaces that resonate with our passions and interests. Volunteering offers a structured way to engage with causes that matter to you, providing a platform to apply your skills and experience in meaningful ways. Consider causes that have tugged at your heartstrings —whether it's mentoring young women entering the workforce or supporting environmental initiatives. These roles can offer personal fulfillment and a chance to contribute positively to society. Community engagement activities further expand this horizon, allowing you to connect with others who share similar interests. Join local clubs or groups focused on gardening, book discussions, or any activity that sparks joy. Engaging with your community in this way enriches your life and builds a network of support and camaraderie.

As we redefine success, shifting our perspective from achieving external accolades to cultivating internal happiness and fulfillment becomes essential. Success is no longer measured by promotions or bonuses but by the joy and satisfaction that come from living authentically. Create new metrics for personal success that reflect your current priorities, such as the quality of your relationships, the depth of your experiences, or your impact on your community. Exploring unconventional success stories can provide inspiration. Consider the story of a woman who became an accomplished writer in her retirement years, using her life experiences as rich material for her novels. Her success wasn't defined by traditional standards but by the fulfillment she found in expressing herself through storytelling.

Interactive Exercise: Defining Your Personal Fulfillment

Take a few moments to jot down what personal fulfillment means to you. List activities or roles that align with your core values and bring you joy. Reflect on how these pursuits might redefine success in your life. Consider how they contribute to your sense of purpose and happiness. Use this exercise as a foundation for exploring new opportunities that resonate with your true self.

The exploration of new possibilities is an exciting aspect of this phase. Retirement offers the freedom to try activities you may have never considered before. Attend workshops or classes on novel subjects that pique your curiosity, whether learning a new language, exploring culinary arts, or diving into digital photography. These experiences provide intellectual stimulation and open doors to new friendships and interests. The key is to approach each opportunity with an open mind and a willingness to embrace the unknown. As you engage with these new activities, you'll find that personal fulfillment is not a destination but a continual process of growth and discovery.

This shift from job titles to personal fulfillment is a transformative process that invites you to explore deeper aspects of yourself. It's about embracing the freedom to pursue what truly matters and finding joy in the everyday moments. As you navigate this transition, remember that personal fulfillment is an ongoing journey that evolves as you do. It's a path where every experience adds richness to your life, painting a picture of success defined by happiness and contentment.

1.3 WRITING YOUR NEXT CHAPTER: PERSONAL DEVELOPMENT PLANS

As you stand on the threshold of retirement, consider the possibilities that lie ahead. This time in your life provides the perfect opportunity to craft a personal development plan—a structured approach to growth that acknowledges your past while embracing your future. Such planning isn't about filling time; it's about enriching your life with purpose and intention. The first step is to outline a clear vision of what you wish to achieve, both in the short and long term. Begin by identifying areas where you want to grow, whether it's learning a new language, mastering a musical instrument, or enhancing your physical fitness. By setting specific, measurable goals, you create a roadmap that guides you toward meaningful accomplishments.

Creating a personal development plan involves more than just listing aspirations. It requires a thoughtful process of goal setting and reflection. Use an outline to break down your goals into actionable steps. This approach clarifies your objectives and makes them feel attainable. For instance, if your goal is to learn French, start with a short-term goal of completing an introductory course. Then, set a long-term goal of traveling to France to practice your skills. Breaking down these goals into smaller, manageable tasks helps maintain focus and motivation. With each step, you build confidence and move closer to realizing your ambitions.

Tracking your progress is essential to personal development. Regularly monitoring your achievements allows you to celebrate successes and identify areas for improvement. Journaling can be an effective tool for self-reflection, offering insights into your journey and helping you adjust your plans as needed. Document your thoughts, challenges, triumphs, and use this record to gain perspective on your growth. Additionally, consider using apps designed for goal tracking. These tools provide reminders, track milestones, and offer a visual representation of your progress, keeping you motivated.

A commitment to lifelong learning is essential for personal development. Engaging in continuing education enhances cognitive function and provides a sense of purpose. This stage of life presents the ideal opportunity to dive into subjects that spark your interest. Whether you enroll in online courses or attend local classes, the wealth of knowledge available is vast and varied. Learning something new, such as playing the piano or taking a cooking class, stimulates the mind and enriches your daily life. This pursuit of knowledge ensures that you remain curious, engaged, and intellectually active.

When setting goals, it's crucial to remain realistic and achievable. The SMART framework—specific, measurable, attainable, relevant, and time-bound—offers a practical method for structuring your objectives. By defining clear parameters, you create a focused path to success. This method encourages setting attainable goals that align with your capabilities and resources. Celebrate your progress along the way, acknowledging each milestone as a victory. These small successes fuel motivation and provide the encouragement needed to pursue larger goals.

1.4 PERSONAL DEVELOPMENT TEMPLATE: SETTING GOALS

Consider using a personal development guide to structure your goals. Start by writing down your long-term aspirations and breaking them into short-term objectives. For each goal, list the specific steps required to achieve it and set a timeline for completion. This guide serves as a map of your journey, keeping you organized and focused. Regularly review and adjust your plan to ensure it remains aligned with your evolving interests and priorities.

Personal development is a lifelong endeavor, one that evolves as you do. By actively pursuing growth, you create a rich and fulfilling retirement experience. This chapter in your life offers the freedom to explore new interests, deepen your knowledge, and cultivate skills that enrich your existence. As you embrace this process, remember that personal development is not about reaching an endpoint but about enjoying the journey of self-discovery and transformation.

1.5 DISCOVERING HIDDEN PASSIONS AND INTERESTS

Imagine a canvas stretched out before you, blank yet brimming with potential. Retirement offers a similar landscape, inviting you to explore hidden passions and interests that may have been over-shadowed by the demands of daily life. Many women find them-selves at this crossroads, eager yet uncertain about where to begin. The first step is to ignite a sense of curiosity about what genuinely excites you. This process starts with brainstorming sessions, where you jot down activities that have always intrigued you—whether it's painting, gardening, or learning the violin. Let your mind wander freely, without judgment or hesitation. This exercise aims to shake off the dust from interests that may have been shelved for decades, waiting patiently for their moment to shine.

Participation in introductory classes can serve as a gentle entry point into these newfound or rediscovered pursuits. Community centers, local colleges, and online platforms offer beginner courses designed to spark interest and nurture skills. These classes provide a structured environment where you can learn at your own pace, surrounded by others who share your excitement. They also serve as a fantastic opportunity to meet like-minded individuals, creating a sense of camaraderie and support. For instance, a pottery class might reveal a natural talent for sculpting, while a photography workshop could reignite a forgotten passion for capturing life's moments. By stepping into these spaces, you open yourself to a world of possibilities, each offering its own unique set of rewards.

Experimentation is key, and this requires courage and a willingness to step outside your comfort zone. The idea is to sample a variety of activities, much like sampling dishes at a buffet, to discover what truly resonates with you. Local workshops and community events often provide hands-on experiences without the commitment of long-term enrollment. These settings allow you to dabble in different hobbies, from salsa dancing to woodworking, without the pressure of mastering them immediately. This process uncovers hidden talents and fosters personal growth. Engaging in these activities can lead to unexpected transformations, as many individuals find a renewed sense of purpose and confidence through hobby exploration. Whether it turns into a lifelong passion or a brief flirtation, each new endeavor adds to the rich mixture of your personal development.

Consider the joy of rediscovering past interests that may have been set aside during your career. Perhaps you once loved to write poetry or play the piano but haven't touched a pen or a key in years. Retirement provides the perfect opportunity to revisit these activities with fresh eyes and renewed enthusiasm. Reconnecting with childhood pastimes can be particularly rewarding, as they often carry a sense of nostalgia and comfort. They remind us of simpler times when creativity flowed freely, unencumbered by the responsibilities of adulthood. By revisiting these interests, you honor your past and enrich your present. They offer a delightful way to fill your days with activities that bring joy and satisfaction.

As you navigate this exploration, keep in mind that discovering hidden passions is not about achieving perfection or even proficiency. It's about finding joy in the process, embracing curiosity, and allowing yourself the freedom to explore without judgment. This stage of life offers the rare gift of time—time to experiment, to play, and to indulge in activities that nurture your soul. Whether you find yourself drawn to painting landscapes, writing memoirs, or simply taking nature walks, let these pursuits guide you toward a fulfilling and engaged lifestyle. The possibilities are endless, each offering its own path to personal enrichment.

1.6 PERSONALITY ASSESSMENTS: TOOLS FOR SELF-DISCOVERY

Imagine having a detailed map that helps you navigate the intricate landscape of your personality, allowing you to uncover layers of yourself you might not have fully understood. Personality assessments offer just that—a tool to delve into the nuances of your character, preferences, and potential. These assessments, like the Myers-Briggs Type Indicator (MBTI) and the Enneagram, provide insights into your personality traits, helping you appreciate your innate strengths and areas for growth. The MBTI categorizes personalities into 16 distinct types based on factors like introversion versus extroversion, while the Enneagram identifies nine interconnected personality types. Understanding these can illuminate why you gravitate toward certain activities or how you approach decision-making. This newfound clarity can be a catalyst for self-acceptance and personal development.

Once you've completed an assessment, the next step is interpreting the results in a meaningful and actionable way. It's not just about reading a report; it's about understanding how the results translate into real-world applications. Consider using worksheets that map your personality traits to potential interests and activities. For example, exploring artistic pursuits or problem-solving workshops might be fulfilling if your assessment reveals a strong preference for creativity and innovation. Community-building activities or group classes could be a perfect fit if you thrive on social interaction. These tools encourage a deeper engagement with your results, transforming abstract concepts into concrete actions that align with your personality.

Understanding your personality can serve as a guidepost when choosing new pursuits, ensuring that your post-retirement activities are both rewarding and aligned with who you are. Take, for instance, someone who discovers through the Enneagram that they are a Type 2, known for their nurturing nature and desire to help others. This insight could lead them to volunteer work in caregiving or mentorship, where they can thrive by supporting and nurturing those around them. By aligning activities with your personality traits, you create a harmonious balance between your inherent tendencies and the new roles you embrace. This alignment often leads to greater satisfaction and a sense of authenticity in your daily life.

Integrating these personality insights into your daily routine is where the real transformation occurs. Knowing your personality type can inform how you structure your day, interact with others, and approach challenges. For instance, an introverted personality might find solace in quiet mornings filled with reflective activities, while an extroverted personality might thrive by scheduling social interactions throughout the day. Tailoring your routines to suit your personality enhances your well-being and optimizes your energy levels and productivity. This personalized approach allows you to engage with the world in a natural and fulfilling way, reducing stress and increasing joy.

Consider famous examples of individuals who have leveraged their personality insights to achieve remarkable things. Think of an artist who, understanding her need for solitude, structured her day around quiet mornings of painting, leading to some of her most profound work. Or a community leader whose extroverted nature drove him to organize successful local events, bringing people together in meaningful ways. These stories remind us that when we honor our personality traits, we unlock potential and possibilities that might otherwise remain dormant.

As you explore the depths of your personality, remember that these assessments are just one part of a larger picture. They provide a foundation for building a life that resonates with your true self. Embrace their insights and allow them to guide you toward activities and roles that fulfill and inspire you.

1.7 CRAFTING YOUR UNIQUE RETIREMENT NARRATIVE

Imagine your life as a book, with each chapter detailing the experiences, lessons, and triumphs that have shaped your journey. Retirement is not the end of this story but the beginning of a new chapter—a blank page ready for your unique narrative. The power of storytelling lies in its ability to clarify and amplify our experiences, offering insight into our past and guiding our future. Writing your retirement story can be a transformative exercise, allowing you to reflect on your life's journey and envision what lies ahead. Start by considering the key moments that have defined your path thus far. What lessons have you learned? What dreams remain unfulfilled? Use these reflections as the foundation for your narrative, crafting a story that captures your hopes, aspirations, and the essence of who you are.

Narrative writing exercises can help you articulate your personal retirement story. Begin by writing a letter to your future self, detailing your vision for this next phase of life. What do you hope to achieve? How do you envision spending your days? This exercise encourages you to think deeply about your goals and aspirations, providing a roadmap for the future. Another approach is to write a short story featuring yourself as the main character. Picture a day in your ideal retirement filled with activities that bring joy and fulfillment. Describe the scenes, characters, and emotions in vivid detail, painting a picture of the life you wish to create. These exercises help you clarify your vision and inspire you to take action toward realizing it.

The power of storytelling extends beyond personal growth; it also fosters connection and inspiration when shared with others. Sharing your narrative opens the door to meaningful conversations, allowing others to learn from your experiences and insights. Consider joining platforms or groups where you can share your story, such as writing clubs, online forums, or community storytelling events. These spaces provide a supportive environment to express your journey, offering encouragement and feedback from like-minded individuals. Sharing your story can also be a source of inspiration for others, demonstrating that retirement is a time of opportunity and growth.

Documenting your journey through journaling or blogging can be a valuable tool for reflection and growth. Keeping a record of your experiences allows you to track your progress, celebrate achievements, and learn from challenges. Writing provides a private space to express thoughts and emotions, offering clarity and perspective. Regular entries can help you stay connected to your goals, fostering a sense of accountability. For those who enjoy a more public platform, blogging offers the chance to share your journey with a broader audience. Blogs can serve as a personal diary and a resource for others seeking guidance and inspiration. Whether you choose to journal privately or blog publicly, documenting your experiences ensures that your narrative continues to evolve and inspire.

1.8 STORYTELLING FRAMEWORK: CRAFTING YOUR PERSONAL NARRATIVE

Consider using a storytelling framework to structure your retirement narrative. Start by identifying the theme or message you wish to convey. Next, outline the key events or experiences that have shaped your journey. Finally, describe your vision for the future, highlighting the goals and aspirations that drive you. Use this framework as a guide to craft a narrative that captures the essence of your retirement story.

In crafting your unique retirement narrative, you create a powerful tool for personal growth and connection. Your story is a reflection of your journey, capturing the challenges you've overcome and the dreams you hold dear. As you embrace this new chapter, allow your narrative to guide and inspire you, reminding you of the endless possibilities that lie ahead. Retirement is not just a phase of life; it's an opportunity to write the next chapter of your story, filled with purpose, joy, and fulfillment.

2

FINANCIAL PEACE OF MIND
WITHOUT HIGH WEALTH

Picture this: Joan, a vibrant 62-year-old, sits at her kitchen table, surrounded by a pile of bills and receipts. She looks at her retirement savings account with a mix of hope and trepidation. Like many women in her age group, Joan is navigating the complex waters of retirement finances, keen to maintain her lifestyle without the cushion of a lavish pension. This chapter is dedicated to women like Joan, who seek financial peace of mind without relying on substantial wealth. It's about creating a roadmap that leads to comfort and security, allowing you to enjoy the fruits of your labor without unnecessary stress.

2.1 BUDGETING FOR A COMFORTABLE LIFESTYLE

Effective budgeting is at the heart of financial peace—a skill that can transform how you manage money during retirement. Envision your budget as a well-crafted recipe, where each ingredient is carefully measured to create a satisfying dish. Begin by understanding the foundational elements of a sustainable retirement budget, which includes distinguishing between fixed and variable expenses. Fixed expenses are your essentials, such as housing, utilities, and healthcare, which remain relatively stable each month. Variable expenses, on the other hand, cover discretionary spending like dining out, travel, and hobbies, which can fluctuate based on your choices.

Tracking these expenses is crucial; thankfully, technology offers several tools to simplify this task. Consider using budgeting apps like YNAB (You Need A Budget) or EveryDollar, which help you monitor spending and make informed financial decisions. These apps provide a user-friendly platform to categorize expenses and visualize your financial landscape. For those who prefer a more traditional approach, spreadsheets can be equally effective, allowing you to customize and adjust as needed. The key is consistency—regularly updating your budget ensures you stay on track and avoid surprises.

Prioritizing needs over wants is essential in crafting a budget that supports a comfortable lifestyle. This involves distinguishing between what's necessary and what's merely desirable. Practical exercises, such as categorizing expenses into "needs" and "wants," can clarify where your money goes and where adjustments can be made. Start by listing all monthly expenses, then assess each item's importance. This exercise not only highlights potential savings but also encourages mindful spending, ensuring your resources align with your values and goals.

Regular budget reviews and adjustments are vital to maintaining financial stability. Life is dynamic, and so should your budget be. Schedule regular strategy sessions—perhaps quarterly or semi-annually—to review your financial situation and make necessary adjustments. This practice allows you to adapt to life changes, such as unexpected medical expenses or shifts in income. During these reviews, assess if your spending aligns with your priorities and if there are areas where you can cut back. Flexibility is your ally, enabling you to respond to financial challenges with confidence and ease.

Living comfortably within your means doesn't mean sacrificing joy or fulfillment. It's about making thoughtful choices that support your desired lifestyle. Consider cost-saving tips like bulk purchasing or energy-saving practices, which can reduce expenses without diminishing your quality of life. For instance, buying non-perishable items in bulk can lead to significant savings over time. Similarly, simple measures like unplugging electronics when not in use or switching to LED lighting can lower utility bills. These strategies demonstrate how minor adjustments can impact your overall budget, allowing you to enjoy retirement with peace of mind.

Practical Exercise: Crafting Your Budget

Take a moment to draft a preliminary budget. List your expenses, such as mortgage or rent, utilities, and insurance. Next, add your variable expenses, like groceries, entertainment, and travel. Use a budgeting app or spreadsheet to categorize and track these expenses over the next month. At the end of the month, review your spending. Identify areas where you can reduce costs and adjust your budget accordingly. This exercise enhances financial awareness and empowers you to make informed decisions, fostering a sense of control and confidence in your financial future.

2.2 SMART SAVING STRATEGIES: MAXIMIZING YOUR INCOME

Imagine a rainy day. The sky darkens, and the gentle patter of raindrops turns into a steady downpour. In financial terms, these unexpected storms are the unforeseen expenses that can unsettle even the most carefully laid plans. Building an emergency fund is like an umbrella for such days—it's your safety net, protecting you from life's unpredictable turns. To establish this fund, calculate three to six months' worth of living expenses. Consider all necessary costs like housing, food, and healthcare. Once you've determined the amount, gradually set aside money until you reach your target. Begin with small, consistent contributions. For example, directly allocate a fixed percentage of any extra income, like tax refunds or bonuses, into your emergency fund. This method ensures you are prepared to face financial challenges with resilience and confidence.

The concept of automatic savings is another invaluable strategy to secure your financial future. Think of it as setting your financial autopilot. By setting up automatic transfers to your savings account, you remove the temptation to spend money on non-essential items. This approach ensures that savings become a priority rather than an afterthought. To implement this, coordinate with your bank to transfer a predetermined amount from your checking account to your savings account each month. Even small amounts add up over time, contributing to a sense of financial stability and peace of mind. This practice simplifies the saving process and cultivates a habit of consistent saving, reinforcing your commitment to financial health.

Though seemingly negligible, daily expenses can accumulate into significant costs over time. By adopting smart strategies, you can reduce these expenses without compromising your quality of life.

Start by embracing couponing and discount shopping. Many retailers offer loyalty programs and coupons, which can lead to substantial savings on everyday purchases. Additionally, consider shopping during sales or exploring generic brands, which often provide similar quality at a lower price. Another effective way to trim costs is through conservation. Turning off lights when leaving a room or using energy-efficient appliances can significantly reduce utility bills. These small changes can lead to noticeable savings, allowing you to allocate funds toward more meaningful endeavors.

Managing and reducing debt is a critical component of maximizing your income. Debt can often feel like a heavy weight, restricting your financial freedom. To address this, create a debt repayment plan. Start by listing all your debts, including interest rates and minimum payments. Prioritize paying off high-interest debts first, as they accumulate the most cost over time. Consider using the snowball method, where you focus on paying off the smallest debt first, then roll the amount into the next smallest debt, creating a momentum that motivates continued progress. Alternatively, the avalanche method targets high-interest debts first for quicker financial relief. Whichever method you choose, the goal is to chip away at your debt consistently, freeing up more income for savings and investments. By actively managing your debt, you can reduce financial stress and create a more straightforward path toward achieving your retirement dreams.

Incorporating these smart saving strategies into your financial routine ensures that you make the most of your resources, regardless of the size of your retirement fund. Whether it's setting up automatic savings, reducing daily expenses, or tackling debt, each step contributes to a more secure and fulfilling retirement. As you implement these practices, you'll find that financial peace is not just about having a significant income but about making wise and deliberate choices with your resources.

2.3 AFFORDABLE INVESTMENT OPTIONS FOR BEGINNERS

Stepping into the world of investing can feel like entering a bustling market with endless stalls, each offering promises of prosperity. For many women approaching or already in retirement, the idea of investing may seem daunting, especially with limited resources. Yet, the landscape of investing has evolved, offering numerous options that are both accessible and affordable. Picture investing as planting a garden: it requires patience, care, and a bit of knowledge about where to place your seeds. One of the most beginner-friendly investment options is low-cost index funds or Exchange-Traded Funds (ETFs). These funds pool money from many investors to purchase a diversified portfolio of stocks or bonds, mirroring a specific index like the S&P 500. By investing in these funds, you're buying into a broad market, which reduces the risk associated with individual stocks. With low expense ratios, these funds are an efficient way to grow your money over time without the need for constant management.

Diversification, a cornerstone of investing, is a safety net for your portfolio. Pretend you are walking a tightrope with a balancing pole; diversification helps you maintain equilibrium by spreading investments across various assets. This strategy mitigates risk because one asset's performance doesn't dictate your entire portfolio's success. A well-diversified portfolio might include a mix of stocks, bonds, and real estate, each contributing differently to your investment goals. Consider the example of a retiree who allocates her savings into a blend of domestic stocks, international bonds, and real estate investment trusts (REITs). This mixture provides stability and opens avenues for growth and income. By diversifying, you shield your investments from market volatility while positioning yourself for long-term success.

In the digital age, investment platforms have become more accessible than ever, opening doors for beginners eager to dip their toes into investing. Online brokerages, such as Robinhood or Charles Schwab, offer user-friendly interfaces with low fees, making it easier for newcomers to navigate the investment waters without feeling overwhelmed. These platforms often provide educational resources, guiding you through the basics of trading and offering insights into market trends. They also allow you to start small, with minimal initial investments, making them ideal for those new to investing. By choosing a platform that suits your comfort level and financial goals, you can begin to build a portfolio that aligns with your vision for retirement.

Starting small and growing your investments is a prudent approach, especially for those new to the investment arena. Think of it as dipping your toes in the water before diving in. This strategy, known as dollar-cost averaging, involves investing a fixed amount of money at regular intervals, regardless of market conditions. By doing so, you buy more shares when prices are low and fewer when prices are high, which can lower the average cost of your investments over time. This method builds discipline and reduces the emotional impact of market fluctuations. Additionally, reinvesting dividends—profits paid out by companies to shareholders—can significantly boost your portfolio's growth. By choosing to reinvest these earnings, you purchase more shares, compounding your investment's growth over time. This approach ensures that your money continues to work for you, even when you're not actively managing it.

As you explore these affordable investment options, remember that investing is a journey of learning and adaptation. It's about finding what works for you and aligning your investments with your financial goals. Start with the basics, embrace the learning process, and gradually expand your investment knowledge. With time, patience, and a bit of curiosity, you'll find that investing can be a rewarding venture that supports a fulfilling and secure retirement.

2.4 NAVIGATING SOCIAL SECURITY AND BENEFITS

Social Security, a foundation of retirement planning, often feels like a complex maze. Yet, understanding its fundamentals can provide a sense of security. Social Security is a government program designed to replace a portion of your income when you retire. Your benefits are calculated based on your 35 highest-earning years. If you worked fewer than 35 years, zeros are factored into the calculation, which can lower your average earnings and, subsequently, your benefits. To qualify, you generally need 40 credits, which you earn through paying Social Security taxes on your earnings. Most people accumulate these credits by working for at least ten years. Once you've reached the eligible age of 62, you can start claiming benefits. However, claiming early results in reduced monthly payouts. Full retirement age varies between 66 and 67, depending on your birth year. Waiting until 70 maximizes your monthly benefits, though not everyone can afford to wait that long.

The application process for claiming Social Security benefits is more straightforward than you might think. The Social Security Administration (SSA) offers an online application that guides you through each step. You'll need personal information, such as your Social Security number, birth certificate, and the names of your spouse and children. It's also wise to gather financial documents, including tax returns, to streamline the process. Once your application is submitted, the SSA will review your information and notify you of your benefit status. Many find the online process convenient, as it allows for tracking progress and receiving updates electronically. If you prefer in-person assistance, visiting a local Social Security office is also an option. However, making an appointment is advisable to avoid long wait times.

Timing is everything when it comes to maximizing your Social Security benefits. One key strategy is delaying your claim. Each year you wait beyond your full retirement age, your benefits increase by a certain percentage until you reach 70. This delay can significantly enhance your monthly income if you have other resources to rely on in the interim. Another approach involves considering spousal benefits. If you're married, divorced, or widowed, you may be eligible for benefits based on your spouse's work record, potentially boosting your overall income. Consulting with a financial advisor can help determine the best strategy for your specific circumstances, ensuring you optimize your benefits based on your unique life situation.

Beyond Social Security, several other programs can support retirees, enhancing financial stability. Medicare, a federal health insurance program, becomes available at age 65, providing coverage for hospital stays, doctor visits, and prescription medications. Understanding the different parts of Medicare—Part A, B, C, and D—can help you choose a plan that suits your healthcare needs. Another government program, Medicaid, assists low-income individuals with medical expenses, supplementing Medicare for those who qualify. Numerous low-income assistance programs also offer support for necessities like food, housing, and energy. These programs can make a substantial difference in your financial well-being, providing relief and peace of mind.

To navigate these benefits effectively, staying informed and proactive is essential. Regularly reviewing your Social Security statement, available online, can help you understand your estimated benefits and plan accordingly. This statement provides a snapshot of your earnings history and the credits you've accumulated, allowing you to verify the accuracy of your records. Additionally, attending workshops or seminars on retirement planning can offer valuable insights into managing your benefits and maximizing your income. These resources empower you to make informed decisions, ensuring that you leverage every available opportunity to secure a comfortable retirement.

2.5 FINANCIAL PLANNING FOR DIVERSE SITUATIONS

Retirement brings a diverse set of financial circumstances for everyone, shaped significantly by personal and family dynamics. Whether you're navigating this phase as a single woman, part of a couple, or within a family structure that includes dependents, your financial planning must reflect these nuances. For singles, the focus often leans towards self-reliance and ensuring that savings and investments cater to individual needs. This might involve a heavier emphasis on building a robust emergency fund and providing comprehensive healthcare coverage. In contrast, couples must navigate joint finances, balancing shared expenses while also accounting for each partner's individual financial goals. This requires open communication and joint decision-making, particularly when planning for large expenditures or long-term care. Families with dependents, such as children or elderly parents, face the added complexity of supporting multiple generations. This can include budgeting for education costs or healthcare needs, requiring careful prioritization and potentially more significant savings goals to accommodate these additional responsibilities.

The unpredictable nature of life means that even the best-laid plans can face disruption. A contingency plan is paramount, whether it is a sudden health issue or an unexpected family event. Start by identifying potential risks and considering how they might impact your financial situation. This could be anything from medical emergencies to natural disasters. Once you've pinpointed these risks, consider the resources you would need to mitigate them. For instance, maintaining a dedicated emergency fund that can cover several months of expenses is a practical step. Additionally, consider your insurance policies—do they adequately cover the potential scenarios you've identified? Ensure your policies are up-to-date and you understand your coverage's specifics. Regularly revisiting these plans ensures they remain relevant as your life circumstances evolve.

Customizing your financial plan to fit your unique situation is crucial. A one-size-fits-all approach rarely works because every-one's financial landscape is different. Use financial worksheets or outlines to map out your specific needs and objectives. These tools help you visualize your financial picture, allowing you to identify areas where adjustments are necessary. For example, if you're experiencing a lifestyle change, such as downsizing your home, your financial plan should reflect this shift. Tailored strategies include reallocating funds to better serve your new goals, whether increasing your savings rate or investing in a new opportunity. The key is regularly reviewing and updating your plan to align with your current and future aspirations.

Seeking professional financial advice can also be wise, especially when navigating complex situations or significant life changes occur. Financial advisors bring expertise that can help you opti-mize your strategy and ensure you're making informed decisions. When choosing an advisor, look for someone with a solid reputa-tion and relevant experience, ideally someone who understands your specific needs and goals. It's important to ask questions about their approach and ensure you feel comfortable with their advice. Many advisors offer a free initial consultation, which can be a good opportunity to assess whether their services align with your expectations. Remember, the goal is to find a partner in your financial planning who can provide clarity and confidence in your retirement strategy.

2.6 CREATIVE WAYS TO SUPPLEMENT YOUR INCOME

As retirement unfolds, the rhythm of daily life changes and opportunities arise to explore new avenues for financial growth. Part-time work and flexible job opportunities are increasingly tailored to fit a retiree's lifestyle, offering the chance to engage with the world while supplementing income. Consider roles in freelancing or consultancy, where your accumulated expertise can be leveraged without the constraints of a full-time role. These positions allow you to work on projects that excite you from the comfort of your home or in settings that suit you. Alternatively, seasonal or part-time employment can provide a steady yet flexible income stream. For instance, working as a seasonal tour guide or a part-time retail assistant during busy periods can add variety to your routine while enhancing your financial stability. These roles provide financial benefits and enhance social interaction, allowing you to remain active and engaged in community life.

Your skills and hobbies, honed over a lifetime, can also become a source of income. Teaching or tutoring in a specialized field allows you to share your knowledge and passion with others. Whether it's offering piano lessons to children or guiding adults through the intricacies of a new language, teaching can be as rewarding financially as it is personally fulfilling. Moreover, the digital age offers platforms that make it easy to reach students worldwide, broadening your impact and income potential. For those with a knack for creativity, selling crafts or homemade goods online presents a lucrative opportunity. Websites like Etsy provide a marketplace for handmade items, enabling you to turn crafting hobbies into a thriving business. Whether you create jewelry, knitwear or home decor, there's a growing market eager to embrace unique, hand-crafted items. This venture supplements income and allows you to express creativity and connect with a community of like-minded artisans.

Passive income opportunities offer another path, one that requires minimal ongoing effort but can yield considerable benefits. Renting out property or space, for instance, can be an excellent way to generate extra income. If you have a spare room, consider listing it on short-term rental sites like Airbnb. Renting out unused storage space or parking areas can also provide a steady income stream for those with unused storage space. Once set up, these arrangements typically require minimal effort, allowing you to enjoy financial returns with low day-to-day involvement. The key to successful passive income is initial planning and setup, after which your assets continue to work for you.

The digital landscape also opens doors to community and online resources that support income generation. Platforms like Fiverr offer a space to promote your freelance services, whether it's graphic design, writing, or digital marketing. These platforms connect you with clients seeking your particular skill set, providing a flexible approach to work that fits your schedule and interests. Joining online marketplaces is another way to reach a wider audience and diversify income opportunities. Notably, these platforms often come with built-in tools for marketing and sales, reducing the need for extensive technical knowledge. This accessibility means you can focus on your strengths and passions, allowing your talents to shine in a global marketplace.

Incorporating these creative income strategies into your retirement plan provides not only financial rewards but also personal satisfaction. By exploring part-time work, leveraging your skills, and tapping into passive income opportunities, you create a diverse financial portfolio that supports a vibrant lifestyle. As we transition to the next chapter, we'll continue to build on these foundations, exploring how to maintain a fulfilling and active retirement that aligns with your goals and aspirations.

3

BUILDING AND MAINTAINING SOCIAL CONNECTIONS

G azing out your window, you might observe the lively flow of life and wonder how to reconnect with its vibrant social threads. Retirement brings the luxury of time, yet it can also introduce a feeling of isolation, a stark shift from the familiar, interaction-rich environment of work to a quieter, more individual lifestyle. This chapter guides you towards rediscovering your sense of community—finding a group that resonates with your interests and lays the groundwork for enduring supportive relationships. It encourages you to venture beyond your usual boundaries, to engage with clubs or groups that bring you joy, and to relish the collective experiences that come from such engagement. On this path of reconnection, you will find the unmatched joy of being part of a community that shares your interests and celebrates life's achievements together.

Joining clubs and groups is like opening the door to a world of camaraderie and support. When you become part of a community, you gain more than just companionship; you find a place to share stories, laughter, and common interests. This sense of belonging can profoundly enhance your social life, providing a network of friends who understand your joys and challenges. Whether it's a book club that meets over coffee or a gardening group that exchanges tips and stories, these gatherings foster connections and kindle friendships that enrich your retirement years. Sharing experiences with others who share your passions can transform ordinary days into extraordinary ones filled with warmth and understanding.

Finding the right club or group starts with identifying what ignites your passion. Contemplate exploring local community centers or libraries, which often host a variety of clubs catering to diverse interests. From knitting or quilting circles to photography classes, these venues offer a treasure trove of activities that can spark joy and engagement. Libraries frequently serve as hubs for educational and social events, providing a welcoming space to meet new people and learn new things. For those who prefer a more tailored approach, online platforms like Meetup offer a gateway to niche groups that align with your personal values and interests. Whether you're drawn to hiking, art, or culinary delights, these platforms connect you with like-minded individuals eager to share their enthusiasm.

The variety of clubs and groups available is as diverse as your interests. Book clubs offer a chance to delve into new worlds through literature, while gardening groups provide the satisfaction of nurturing life and sharing the fruits of your labor. Art classes let you explore creativity and self-expression, offering a supportive environment to try new techniques and hone your skills. Each group provides a unique opportunity to expand your horizons and form connections based on shared passions. Joining these clubs fills your calendar with engaging activities and introduces you to a community of individuals who enrich your experience with diverse perspectives and stories.

Active participation in these groups is key to fostering deeper connections. Attending meetings is a start, but taking an active role can transform your experience. Volunteering for leadership roles or organizing group activities allows you to shape the group's direction and create memorable events. By stepping into these roles, you contribute to the group's success and strengthen your ties with fellow members. Organizing a book club meeting or planning a garden tour encourages collaboration and creativity, strengthening bonds and a sense of accomplishment. Active involvement ensures you are not just a spectator but an integral part of your community, where your contributions are valued and friendships flourish.

Reflection Exercise: Mapping Your Social Interests

Think about taking a moment to reflect on your interests. Grab a pen and paper and list activities you've always wanted to try or deepen your involvement. Think about the skills you have and how they might contribute to a club or group. Reflect on what you hope to gain from these interactions—whether it's learning something new, meeting new people, or simply enjoying a hobby. This exercise helps you identify potential paths and set intentions for building meaningful social connections.

Finding your tribe adds a vibrant layer to your retirement, offering companionship and a sense of purpose. As you explore these connections, you'll discover that being part of a community brings a wealth of experiences, friendships, and opportunities for growth. Welcome the chance to join clubs and groups and watch as your social circle expands, enveloping you in a warm embrace of shared interests and joyful interactions.

3.1 VIRTUAL COMMUNITIES: CONNECTING IN THE DIGITAL AGE

Regard the digital landscape, a vibrant realm where friendships blossom and communities thrive, all from the comfort of your home. Virtual communities have become a lifeline for many, offering a space to connect, share, and grow beyond geographical constraints. In today's world, platforms like Facebook and LinkedIn serve as gateways to these digital circles, providing a space where you can engage with others who share your interests and passions. Whether it's a Facebook group dedicated to gardening or a LinkedIn community for lifelong learners, these platforms foster a sense of belonging and connection that transcends physical boundaries. Through digital interaction, you can participate in conversations, share experiences, and build relationships with people from all corners of the globe, enriching your social life in ways you might not have considered.

Selecting the right online platform is crucial to maximizing the benefits of virtual communities. Start by giving thought to your interests and the type of interaction you seek. Are you looking for professional networking, casual socializing, or a mix of both? Platforms with user-friendly interfaces can make your online experience more enjoyable and less daunting. For instance, Facebook's intuitive design allows you to easily navigate through groups, while LinkedIn offers a more structured environment for professional engagement. Interest-based communities provide tailored spaces where you can delve into specific topics, whether it's a niche hobby or a broader subject like wellness. Evaluating these features will help you find a platform that aligns with your preferences, ensuring a fulfilling and engaging experience.

Digital connections offer unparalleled flexibility and accessibility, enabling you to maintain friendships and participate in activities regardless of your location. You can join global interest groups that connect you with people who share your passions, learn from diverse perspectives, and stay updated on the latest trends. Virtual meetups and webinars allow you to attend events and workshops from your living room, offering opportunities for learning and interaction without the need for travel. This convenience means that you can engage with your community on your terms, fitting social activities around your schedule and commitments. Whether participating in a virtual book club or attending a live cooking class, the digital world opens doors to experiences that keep your social life dynamic and enriching.

As you navigate these digital spaces, it's essential to prioritize your privacy and security. Social media platforms offer various privacy controls that help protect your personal information. Take the time to familiarize yourself with these settings, adjusting them to suit your comfort level. Ensure your profile is visible only to those you trust and be cautious about sharing sensitive information. Engaging with content thoughtfully and staying informed about platform features can also enhance your online experience. Regularly reviewing your privacy settings and understanding how to report inappropriate content are proactive steps that empower you to stay safe online. By maintaining these safeguards, you can enjoy the benefits of virtual communities while protecting your digital footprint.

3.2 MAINTAINING LONG-DISTANCE FRIENDSHIPS

Imagine the joy of hearing the voice of an old friend, the laughter bridging the miles between you. In retirement, nurturing long-distance friendships becomes even more vital. These connections offer a sense of continuity and comfort, reminding you of shared memories and experiences. Regular phone calls or video chats can rekindle the warmth of those relationships, allowing you to share stories, offer support, and celebrate milestones together. A simple call can turn an ordinary day into a special one, bringing familiar voices and cherished moments into your home. Establishing a routine for these calls—perhaps a weekly or bi-weekly chat—creates anticipation and maintains the bond that distance might otherwise strain.

Overcoming the barriers of distance requires creativity and intention. While technology offers many solutions, receiving a handwritten letter or a thoughtfully curated care package is profoundly personal. These tangible tokens of friendship carry a piece of your presence, a reminder of the connection that transcends miles. Visualize the delight of opening a package filled with favorite teas, a book you both discussed, or a small craft you made. Such gestures speak volumes, reinforcing that your friend holds a special place in your heart despite the distance. Additionally, coordinating virtual activities like movie nights or book discussions can bridge the gap, creating shared experiences that mimic those enjoyed in person. Selecting a film to watch simultaneously or reading the same novel opens avenues for conversation and shared reflection.

In today's digital age, technology serves as both a bridge and a lifeline for maintaining friendships separated by geography. Apps like WhatsApp or Skype make it easy to stay in touch through text, voice, and video calls. These tools allow you to see each other's expressions, hear the nuances in your voices, and engage in real-time dialogue. They foster an immediacy and intimacy that letter-writing alone cannot capture. Whether it's a spontaneous video call to share a recent happening or a planned conversation to catch up on each other's lives, these platforms keep the lines of communication open and dynamic. They enable you to celebrate birthdays, holidays, and even daily victories together, nurturing the friendship with regular interaction.

Shared experiences create lasting memories and deepen connections, even when friends are miles apart. Planning joint vacations or meetups can turn anticipation into reality, providing opportunities to explore new places and enjoy each other's company. Picture a weekend getaway to a charming town you've always wanted to visit or a reunion at a favorite vacation spot. These trips become more than just a chance to see each other; they are adventures that build new memories, enhancing the fabric of your friendship. Even if such visits are infrequent, the planning and anticipation can keep the friendship vibrant and engaging, offering a goal to look forward to and a reward for the patience and effort invested in maintaining the relationship. By blending technology with personal gestures and shared experiences, your long-distance friendships can flourish, providing joy, support, and continuity throughout your retirement years.

3.3 HOSTING GATHERINGS: BRINGING PEOPLE TOGETHER

Imagine the warmth of a room filled with laughter, the clinking of glasses, and the soft hum of conversation. Hosting gatherings is more than just bringing people together; it's about weaving a tapestry of relationships that can enrich your life. Opening your home to friends and neighbors creates a hub of connection and camaraderie. These gatherings build a network of local friends, offering a sense of community that many retirees seek. Hosting allows you to rekindle old friendships while forging new ones, transforming acquaintances into lifelong companions. It's not just about the event itself but the lasting bonds formed that continue to grow and flourish over time.

Planning a successful gathering requires creativity and organization, ensuring everyone feels welcome and included. Consider hosting theme-based parties, which can add an element of excitement and cohesiveness to your gathering. Whether it's a 70s disco night or a tropical luau, themes encourage guests to engage and participate actively. Potlucks are another great option, allowing everyone to contribute a dish and share in the communal experience. This eases the burden of preparation and introduces a delightful variety of flavors and dishes. Setting a comfortable and welcoming atmosphere is key; think ambient lighting, cozy seating arrangements, and background music that encourages conversation. Small touches like these create an inviting environment where guests feel at ease.

Let your creativity shine when planning events that are memorable and unique. An outdoor picnic on a sunny afternoon can offer a refreshing change from indoor gatherings, allowing guests to enjoy nature while socializing. Reflect on organizing a game night where friendly competition and laughter can break the ice and strengthen bonds. These unique gatherings entertain and provide an opportunity for guests to interact in different settings, fostering more profound connections. Encourage guests to bring along games or activities they enjoy, creating a collaborative atmosphere that enhances the experience. The key is to encourage creative thinking and tailor events to the interests and preferences of your friends, ensuring a personalized and memorable gathering.

Regularly hosting events can sustain and nurture relationships, keeping friendships vibrant and active. Establishing a routine, such as monthly or quarterly gatherings, creates a rhythm that friends can look forward to, providing continuity and anticipation. These regular meet-ups serve as touchpoints, allowing friends to catch up, share updates, and strengthen bonds. Over time, these gatherings become cherished traditions, etched into the social calendar. They offer a sense of stability and belonging, where everyone knows they have a place to connect and unwind. By committing to regular hosting, you cultivate a supportive network that enriches your retirement and ensures your social circle remains lively and engaged.

The process of hosting and planning these gatherings is as rewarding as the events themselves. It provides an opportunity to express your personality and creativity, whether through the choice of theme, menu, or decorations. Moreover, it allows you to practice and refine organizational, communication, and hospitality skills. As you plan each event, you'll become more adept at anticipating the needs and preferences of your guests, ensuring that each gathering is a success. This sense of accomplishment is deeply satisfying, reinforcing the value and importance of maintaining social connections.

3.4 EMBRACING VOLUNTEERISM: GIVING BACK AND MAKING FRIENDS

Envision standing shoulder to shoulder with a group of enthusiastic individuals, all united by a common goal to make a difference. Volunteering provides a unique opportunity to give back to your community and forge meaningful connections. Engaging in community service projects immerses you in environments where camaraderie and collaboration thrive. These settings offer fertile ground for developing friendships based on shared values and experiences. Whether painting a community center, organizing a charity event, or mentoring young students, each act of service brings you closer to others equally passionate about creating positive change.

For retirees, the benefits of volunteering extend far beyond the immediate impact on society. It's a powerful way to rediscover a sense of purpose and belonging, which can sometimes wane after leaving the workforce. Volunteering fills your days with meaningful activities that engage you mentally and physically. The satisfaction derived from contributing to the well-being of others fosters a profound sense of fulfillment. This active participation in community life can significantly enhance your emotional well-being as you witness firsthand the results of your efforts and the smiles on the faces of those you help. Moreover, volunteering often introduces you to diverse groups of people, enriching your social circle with new friendships and perspectives.

Finding the right volunteer opportunity involves aligning your skills and interests with the needs of the community. Weigh starting with local charities, hospitals, or schools, as these organizations often seek volunteers for a variety of roles. Think about what you enjoy and where your strengths lie. Are you passionate about education? Mentoring students or assisting in a literacy program would be rewarding. If you have a knack for organization, helping with event planning or administrative tasks might suit you. By selecting roles that resonate with your interests, you will more likely find satisfaction and joy in your volunteer work. Take the time to research different organizations and visit them if possible. This allows you to get a feel for their environment and culture, ensuring a good fit for your talents and enthusiasm.

Once you're involved in a volunteer group, building connections with fellow volunteers enhances the experience. Participation in team-building activities strengthens the group dynamic and fosters trust and collaboration. These activities include workshops, training sessions, or informal gatherings where volunteers can unwind and share stories. Such interactions create a sense of community within the group, where everyone works towards a common goal. Sharing personal stories and experiences is another powerful way to bond with other volunteers. These exchanges reveal the motivations and passions that drive each person, deepening mutual understanding and respect. As you open up to others, you'll find that your volunteer group becomes more than just a team—it becomes a network of friends who support and inspire one another.

Volunteering serves as a gateway to enriching social connections and fosters personal growth. When you dedicate your time to community service, you're not just positively impacting those around you; you're also infusing your life with a sense of renewed purpose and companionship. Each volunteer opportunity you accept enriches your social life, adding vibrancy and richness to your journey through retirement. The connections you forge in these settings are rooted in mutual interests and collaborative efforts, leading to meaningful and enduring friendships. These friendships extend well beyond the confines of any single project, creating a supportive network that bolsters your social experiences and magnifies the positive impact you have within your community. Through volunteering, you engage in a reciprocal exchange—offering your skills and time while simultaneously receiving the gift of enriched social interactions and the joy of contributing to the greater good. This dynamic interplay enhances your sense of belonging and purpose, transforming volunteerism into a cornerstone of a fulfilling retirement.

3.5 INTERGENERATIONAL CONNECTIONS: LEARNING AND SHARING ACROSS AGES

Imagine sitting with your grandchildren, their eyes wide with curiosity as you share tales from your past. In return, they teach you the latest dance craze or how to navigate a new app. These moments of exchange are more than just pleasant afternoons; they are the heart of intergenerational connections. Engaging with different age groups enriches your life, offering perspectives and knowledge you might never encounter otherwise. Younger generations bring fresh ideas and insights, introducing you to technology and trends that seem daunting yet exciting. They offer a glimpse into a rapidly changing world, keeping you informed and engaged. This exchange is mutually beneficial as you pass on wisdom and life experiences, providing context and understanding that only years can bring. Sharing stories from their youth or offering career advice based on decades of experience helps them navigate their own journeys with confidence.

Creating opportunities for these intergenerational exchanges can be both simple and deeply rewarding. Give thought to joining programs or workshops designed to bridge age gaps. Many communities offer intergenerational initiatives that bring together people of different ages for mutual learning and interaction. These might include tech classes where younger participants teach seniors how to use smartphones or creative workshops where skills like knitting or painting are shared. Hosting events that welcome all age groups is another avenue. Birthday parties, holiday gatherings, or even casual family dinners can become rich environments for exchange when everyone is encouraged to interact and share. These settings foster an atmosphere where everyone feels valued and included, enhancing the bonds that unite family and community.

The benefits of intergenerational connections extend beyond the immediate joy of companionship. Younger and older individuals have much to teach each other, creating a continuous loop of learning and growth. For younger people, interacting with those who have lived through different times provides historical context and perspective. They gain insight into how past challenges were overcome, learning resilience and adaptability. Meanwhile, older adults are inspired by the energy and enthusiasm of youth, which can reignite their own passions and curiosities. This dynamic enriches your personal growth, offering new angles and insights that keep you mentally agile and emotionally fulfilled.

Mentorship programs offer a structured way to deepen these connections, fostering bonds that can last a lifetime. By providing guidance and support to younger individuals, you become a beacon of knowledge and encouragement. Whether through formal programs or informal arrangements, mentoring allows you to share your expertise, helping others navigate their paths with greater ease. It's more than imparting knowledge; it's about building relationships grounded in trust and mutual respect. These bonds enrich the lives of those you mentor and your own, providing a sense of purpose and connection that transcends generations.

Intergenerational relationships are a mainstay of a vibrant, fulfilling life, offering countless opportunities for growth and connection. As you welcome these bonds, you'll find your own life enriched with new ideas, experiences, and friendships. This chapter, focused on building and maintaining social connections, highlights the importance of diverse relationships. They form the fabric of a life well-lived, providing joy, support, and continued learning. As we move forward, mull over how these connections can be nurtured and expanded, enhancing not only your retirement but the lives of those around you.

4

CREATING A FULFILLING DAILY ROUTINE

As the early morning sun casts shades of pink and gold across the sky, a realization envelops me: retirement transcends just time passing—it's an invitation to savor and celebrate each unfolding moment. This chapter of life unfurls like a blank canvas, ripe with the promise of infusing our days with the possibilities of purpose, joy, and promise. Yet, navigating the balance between peacefulness and active engagement presents its unique set of challenges. Transitioning from the rigid schedule of a career-driven existence to the freedom of an unstructured day can stir a range of emotions, from exhilaration to apprehension, in many women. It underscores the significance of crafting a daily routine that doesn't just aim for fulfillment but becomes an essential foundation for nurturing our overall well-being and happiness.

4.1 THE ART OF BALANCING RELAXATION AND ACTIVITY

Achieving a harmonious balance between relaxation and activity is fundamental to a fulfilling life, particularly as you navigate the transition into retirement. Contemplate your daily routine, where each task and pause contributes to your inner rhythm. This balance serves to skillfully direct the flow of your day—alternating between periods of activity and rest to craft a rhythm that sustains your energy and lifts your spirits. Integrating downtime into your schedule is crucial. This downtime allows your mind and body the essential opportunity to rejuvenate. Picture yourself in a serene moment with a warm cup of tea in your hands, taking the time to pause, take a deep breath, and engage in introspective reflection. These intentional pauses are the keystones in maintaining your enthusiasm for life and keeping your energy levels high throughout your day. By consciously planning these moments of rest, you ensure that each day unfolds in a balanced and meaningful way, allowing you to seize the vibrant days of retirement life with zest and joy.

Incorporating varied activities into your routine adds a layer of interest and engagement, preventing monotony. Engaging in a mix of physical and mental activities stimulates your mind and enhances your overall well-being. Think about joining a local art class or hosting a movie or game night, where you can connect with others while exploring your interests. These activities provide an outlet for creativity and social interaction, enriching your life with new experiences and friendships. Participating in community classes or workshops keeps you active and engaged, contributing to your physical health and emotional happiness.

Relaxation, however, is not merely the absence of activity; it is a deliberate practice that rejuvenates. Meditation and quiet reflection offer sanctuary from the hustle, fostering inner peace and clarity. Try incorporating short meditation sessions into your day, allowing yourself to return to the present moment. Techniques such as deep breathing exercises can further reduce stress and promote serenity. Imagine closing your eyes, taking a deep breath, and feeling tension melt away with each exhale. These moments of stillness are invaluable, providing a foundation of serenity upon which to build your day.

Adaptability is a crucial component of a fulfilling routine, ensuring that your schedule remains flexible and responsive to your needs. Life is fluid and so should your daily activities be. Listen to your body and mind, adjusting your plans based on your energy levels and mood. There will be days when you feel invigorated and ready to tackle new challenges and others when you crave quiet and reflection. Embrace this variability, allowing yourself the grace to shift gears as needed. By honoring your natural rhythms, you craft a routine that supports your well-being and enhances your quality of life.

Interactive Exercise: Crafting Your Daily Balance

Take a moment to reflect on your current daily routine. Identify the activities that invigorate you and those that calm you. Create a simple chart listing these activities under two columns: "Energizing" and "Relaxing." Review how you might balance these elements throughout your day. Use this chart as a guide to design a routine that incorporates both serenity and pursuits, ensuring a harmonious flow. Adjust as needed, keeping in mind that flexibility is key to maintaining balance and joy.

Finding this balance between tranquility and recreation cultivates a lifestyle that nurtures every aspect of one's being. Each day becomes an opportunity to engage with the world while honoring one's needs and desires. One can unlock the potential for a joyful and fulfilling retirement as one receives this art of balance, one day at a time.

4.2 MORNING RITUALS: SETTING A POSITIVE TONE FOR THE DAY

The morning, often seen as the foundation of our day, holds the power to shape our mood and productivity. Ponder waking up not to the blare of an alarm but to the gentle glow of dawn filtering through your curtains. This peaceful start sets the stage for a day filled with intention and purpose. Establishing a soothing morning routine can transform how you approach the hours ahead. By creating a space free from rush, you allow yourself the luxury of easing into the day, your mind quiet and open to possibilities. It's about beginning with intention, where each action feels deliberate and meaningful, setting a positive tone that resonates throughout your daily activities.

Consider incorporating a few simple practices that can help set a positive tone. Gentle morning stretches or a short yoga routine can awaken your body and mind, promoting flexibility and circulation. Picture yourself on a mat, moving through poses that energize and soothe, grounding you in the present moment. Follow this with a nourishing breakfast, perhaps a plate of scrambled eggs with half an avocado brimming with nutrients. This meal fuels your body and signals the beginning of a day in which health and well-being are prioritized. When performed consistently, these rituals become anchors that ground you, providing tranquility amid the day's demands.

Personalization is key to creating a morning routine that truly resonates. Each of us has unique needs and preferences, so tailor your rituals to reflect what brings you joy and peace. For some, it might be journaling, where you jot down goals or intentions for the day. Others might find solace in a quiet corner with a cup of coffee, lost in thought, or immersed in a favorite book. The goal is to craft a routine that feels as natural as breathing and aligns with your rhythm and desires. By listening to what your heart and mind crave, you create a practice that nurtures and inspires, making mornings a time you look forward to with anticipation.

Consistency in morning habits is where the magic truly unfolds. Regularity breeds familiarity, which in turn fosters comfort and ease. Establishing a fixed wake-up time can work wonders for your internal clock, improving sleep quality and ensuring you greet each day refreshed. This consistency becomes a comforting ritual; a familiar friend greets you each morning with reassurance and steadiness. As you repeat these practices, they weave into the fabric of your daily life, bolstering your resilience and enhancing your mood. Over time, the cumulative effect of a consistent morning routine manifests in greater clarity, focus, and a sense of well-being that permeates every aspect of your life.

Reflection Exercise: Crafting Your Morning Ritual

Take a moment to reflect on what you need to start your day off right. Think about activities that invigorate and soothe you, and list them on paper. Reflect on experimenting with different elements—perhaps combining stretches with a healthy breakfast or journaling with meditation or prayer. Over the next week, try incorporating these elements into your morning. Pay attention to how each practice makes you feel and adjust as needed. This exercise allows you to create a personalized morning routine that sets a positive tone for your day, helping you step into each morning with confidence and joy.

4.3 TIME MANAGEMENT TECHNIQUES FOR RETIREES

In retirement, time becomes a vast landscape filled with possibilities yet managing it effectively can be more challenging than expected. While exciting, this newfound freedom requires a thoughtful approach to ensure each day is productive and fulfilling. Think of time management as the compass guiding you through this landscape, helping you prioritize tasks and maximize accomplishments. By identifying what's truly important, you can direct your energy towards activities that enrich your life. Prioritizing doesn't mean filling every single minute with tasks; it means recognizing what matters most and focusing on those elements. Whether it's pursuing a passion or spending time with loved ones, knowing your priorities ensures that your days are spent in alignment with your values.

Achieving this alignment calls for strategies to organize and plan your time efficiently. Give thought to using planners or digital tools to schedule activities, providing a visual roadmap of your day. These tools help you allocate time effectively, ensuring that essential tasks are completed without encroaching on moments meant for leisure or creativity. Setting daily or weekly objectives can further enhance this process, offering clear targets to work towards. By breaking larger goals into manageable pieces, you avoid feeling overwhelmed, making it easier to maintain focus and motivation. This structured approach keeps you on track and fosters a sense of accomplishment as you check off each task, reinforcing the satisfaction of a day well spent.

Beyond structuring your time, setting boundaries is crucial in protecting your personal space and ensuring that your schedule reflects your priorities. Learning to say no to non-essential commitments can be liberating, freeing you from obligations that drain your energy. It's about recognizing that your time is valuable and choosing to spend it in ways that nourish you. This might mean declining an invitation that doesn't excite you or setting limits on volunteer work. By establishing these boundaries, you carve out time for activities that genuinely fulfill you, whether enjoying a quiet afternoon with a book or exploring a new hobby. Protecting your time in this way is an act of self-care, creating space for rest and rejuvenation.

Regularly reviewing and adjusting your schedule is another vital aspect of effective time management. Life is dynamic, and so are your needs and interests. You can identify patterns and make necessary adjustments by assessing how you spend your time. Consider setting aside a moment each week for reflection, examining how your time has been used and what changes might enhance your routine. This practice improves efficiency and ensures your schedule remains flexible and responsive to your evolving goals. It's about finding a rhythm that suits you, allowing for spontaneity and adaptation as needed. This approach fosters a sense of empowerment as you actively shape your days to align with your desires and aspirations.

Effective time management is not about rigid schedules or constant productivity; it's about creating a life that reflects your values and passions. By prioritizing tasks, utilizing planning tools, setting boundaries, and regularly reviewing your schedule, you cultivate a routine that supports your well-being and enriches your retirement experience. Each day becomes an opportunity to fully engage with life, embracing responsibilities and joys with intention and grace.

4.4 INCORPORATING LEARNING AND PERSONAL GROWTH

In the unfolding tapestry of retirement, continuous learning emerges as a vibrant thread, weaving through days with a promise of discovery and growth. Envision the excitement of exploring new subjects, each a doorway to previously unseen worlds. Online courses have transformed this exploration, offering a wealth of knowledge at your fingertips. Whether diving into the mysteries of ancient history or unraveling the complexities of modern technology, these courses invite you to challenge your mind and expand your horizons. The flexibility of online learning means you can engage at your own pace, fitting education seamlessly into the rhythm of your life. This ongoing education isn't just about acquiring new skills; it's about nurturing a curious and agile mind that eagerly adapts to the changing world.

To make learning a joyful part of your daily routine, consider setting aside dedicated time for reading or research. Picture a cozy nook where you can escape into the pages of a gripping novel or delve into an enlightening article. This space becomes a sanctuary for your mind, inviting you to pause, reflect, and absorb. Joining groups and clubs adds a social dimension to your learning, offering opportunities to share insights and engage in stimulating discussions. These gatherings become fertile ground for new ideas and friendships, enriching your life with knowledge and connection. The act of learning transforms from a solitary pursuit to a communal experience, where shared curiosity fosters a sense of belonging and mutual support.

Setting learning goals provides direction and motivation, guiding your educational endeavors with purpose. Think of these goals as milestones on a path of personal development, each a step towards greater understanding and fulfillment. Creating a learning plan with clear objectives helps you focus your efforts, ensuring that your studies align with your interests and aspirations. This plan acts as a roadmap, highlighting the skills you wish to acquire and the subjects you would like to explore. As you achieve each milestone, take a moment to celebrate your progress, acknowledging the growth and confidence that comes from reaching your goals. These celebrations reinforce your commitment to lifelong learning, encouraging you to continue pursuing knowledge with enthusiasm and curiosity.

Curiosity is a powerful catalyst for personal growth, propelling you towards new experiences and insights. Cultivating a mindset of exploration and inquiry invites you to view the world with wonder, seeking out opportunities to learn and grow. This curiosity becomes a guiding light, illuminating paths that lead to new skills and hobbies. Encouraging experimentation opens doors to unexpected passions, transforming routine days into adventures of discovery. Whether trying your hand at painting, learning to play a musical instrument, or experimenting with new culinary creations, each hobby becomes an opportunity to expand your abilities and enrich your life. Welcome the joy of learning for its own sake, allowing your curiosity to lead you to places you've never been before.

Interactive Element: Creating Your Learning Plan

Take a moment to reflect on areas of interest you've always wanted to explore. Jot down subjects or skills that intrigue you and rank them based on your enthusiasm. Next, create a simple learning plan by setting a timeline for each subject, identifying resources, and outlining small goals. This plan serves as your guide, helping you stay focused and motivated as you embark on your educational pursuits. Periodically review and adjust your plan, celebrating each milestone you achieve along the way.

Incorporating learning and personal growth into your daily life transforms retirement into a vibrant engagement and self-discovery period. Each new subject you explore, and every skill you acquire adds depth and richness to your experience, fostering a sense of fulfillment and joy. Through learning, you remain active in the ever-evolving world, your mind is open to possibilities, and your spirit is invigorated by the thrill of discovery.

4.5 DESIGNING YOUR PERFECT DAY: A STEP-BY-STEP GUIDE

Imagine waking up to a day that unfolds precisely as you desire, where relaxation, activity, and personal fulfillment are perfectly balanced. Visualizing your ideal day can be powerful, offering a glimpse into what truly matters to you. Begin by picturing a morning that energizes you, perhaps with a peaceful walk or a cozy moment with your favorite book. Let your mind wander through the afternoon, filled with activities that spark joy—maybe a painting class or a leisurely lunch with a friend. As evening approaches, think about winding down with a serene ritual, like a warm bath, meditation, or prayer. This visualization clarifies your desires and sets the stage for turning them into reality.

Once you have a clear picture of your perfect day, it's time to translate that vision into a structured plan. Reflect on using templates for daily schedule planning to help you organize your time effectively. These templates serve as a guide, allowing you to allocate specific time slots for various activities. Incorporating a mix of activities is crucial to maintaining balance. For instance, blend physical exercise with creative pursuits, ensuring your day caters to both body and mind. This structured approach helps prevent the day from slipping away unnoticed, ensuring that each moment is purposeful and enriching.

It's essential to accept trial and error as part of designing your routine. Life is dynamic, and what works one week might need adjustment the next. Keeping a diary of daily experiences can be incredibly beneficial in refining your schedule. Note what felt satisfying and what seemed off. Did a particular task feel rushed? Was there enough time for relaxation? Use these reflections to tweak your routine, adapting to what feels right. This process is not about perfection but finding a rhythm that suits you. With each adjustment, you gain insight into what truly enhances your daily life.

Customizing your daily schedule is vital, as it ensures your routine aligns with your unique needs and preferences. Tailor your activities based on your energy levels and interests. Some of us are morning people, brimming with energy at dawn, while others find their stride in the afternoon. Recognizing these patterns allows you to schedule more demanding tasks when you feel most alert and reserve quieter activities for when your energy wanes. Personalizing your day this way boosts productivity and enhances your sense of fulfillment, as each day reflects who you are and what you value.

Designing your perfect day isn't about rigidly adhering to a plan but creating a framework supporting your goals and desires. Visualizing your ideal day, planning with intention, experimenting, and customizing your routine are all steps that guide you toward a more fulfilling and balanced life. As you explore these strategies, remember that your daily routine is a canvas, ready to be painted with the colors of your choosing, reflecting the life you aspire to lead.

4.6 EVENING REFLECTIONS: ENDING THE DAY WITH GRATITUDE

As the sun dips below the horizon, casting a warm glow over the day you've lived, take a moment to pause and reflect. Evening reflection is more than a ritual; it's a chance to acknowledge the day's experiences and cultivate a sense of gratitude. This practice can significantly enhance your well-being, as it encourages you to focus on the positives, no matter how small they may seem. Writing about positive experiences and achievements is one way to engage in this reflection. By writing down what went well, you reinforce those experiences in your mind, fostering a sense of accomplishment and contentment. Putting pen to paper transforms fleeting moments into tangible memories, allowing you to revisit them whenever you need a reminder of the good in your life.

Study incorporating mindfulness exercises that promote gratitude and appreciation to deepen your evening reflections. Writing a gratitude list before bed can be particularly effective. List three things you're thankful for—perhaps the laughter shared with a friend, the beauty of a sunset, or the satisfaction of completing a project. This practice shifts your focus from what might be lacking to what you cherish, filling your heart with warmth as you prepare for rest. Meditation or prayer can also enhance your evening routine. Imagine closing your eyes, taking slow, deliberate breaths, and allowing the day's tensions to melt away. These methods help quiet the mind, paving the way for a restful night's sleep.

Creating a peaceful bedtime routine is another essential aspect of gracefully winding down your day. Guide yourself into decompressing by establishing rituals that soothe and calm. Ponder reading a few pages of a favorite book or listening to soothing music that gently lulls you into tranquility. These activities signal to your mind and body that it's time to transition from the day's busyness to the quiet of the night. Setting a consistent bedtime further supports this transition, as it helps regulate your sleep cycle, ensuring you wake up refreshed and ready to embrace a new day. A well-established routine improves sleep quality and contributes to stability and well-being.

Reflecting on the day's events provides an opportunity for personal growth and self-awareness. As you review what transpired, consider both your accomplishments and areas where you might improve. This analysis isn't about self-criticism but about understanding and learning. What moments brought joy? What challenges did you face, and how did you respond? By examining these aspects, you gain insights into your behaviors and choices, equipping you to make more informed decisions in the future. This practice of evening reflection fosters a cycle of continuous growth, where each day's experiences build upon the last, guiding you toward a more fulfilling and mindful life.

As you explore these evening practices, remember that they are meant to enhance your routine, not complicate it. Choose activities that resonate with you and allow them to evolve as your needs change. The goal is to create a space where reflection and gratitude become natural parts of your day, setting the stage for peaceful rest and renewed energy. By ending each day with gratitude, you cultivate a mindset that appreciates life's simple joys, enriching your retirement with a sense of purpose and satisfaction.

Thus, concludes Chapter 4, inviting you to incorporate these insights into your daily life. By embracing these routines, you will create a lifestyle that balances reflection with action, rest with engagement, and solitude with connection. In the next chapter, we will explore how to build and maintain meaningful relationships, continuing to enrich this vibrant phase of life.

SHARE YOUR VOICE, INSPIRE A JOURNEY

THE GIFT OF ENCOURAGEMENT

"The best way to find yourself is to lose yourself in the service of others."

— *MAHATMA GANDHI*

Every act of generosity creates a ripple. By sharing your experience, you could brighten someone else's path.

Would you help a fellow woman ready to redefine her retirement?

My mission with *Retirement Redefined for Women* is to empower women to embrace this new chapter of life with confidence, purpose, and joy. But to reach even more women, I need your help.

Most readers pick their next book based on reviews. By leaving a review, you can help someone who might be feeling overwhelmed or uncertain find the guidance they need to create the life they dream of.

Your review could make all the difference, helping one more woman:

- Find clarity in her retirement vision.
- Build meaningful connections that enrich her life.
- Discover new passions and a renewed sense of purpose.
- Face this chapter of life with courage and confidence.

It takes less than a minute, but your thoughtful words could transform someone's journey.

To share your review and make a difference, simply scan the QR code below:

Thank you for being a part of this community and helping spread the message of empowerment and possibility. Your kindness inspires me and so many others.

With gratitude,

Victoria Spring

5

EXPLORING PURPOSEFUL ENGAGEMENT AND NEW OPPORTUNITIES

I magine the quiet thrill of rediscovering a long-forgotten hobby, like finding a favorite book tucked away on a dusty shelf. For many women entering retirement, this chapter of life opens the door to pursuits that once brought joy but were set aside amid professional and familial commitments. Now is the perfect time to dust off those passions and explore new ones. Engaging in hobbies enriches your days and offers a therapeutic retreat from the hustle of daily life. As you delve into these pursuits, you'll find they can bring a profound sense of fulfillment and serenity.

Hobbies have a remarkable way of lifting spirits and alleviating stress. Examine the calming nature of painting, where each brushstroke becomes a meditative practice. The canvas offers a space to express emotions, transforming them into vibrant colors and shapes. Similarly, pottery invites you to mold and shape with your hands, grounding you in the present moment. These creative outlets serve as a form of mindfulness, allowing you to focus entirely on the task at hand. Such activities have been shown to reduce stress and anxiety, promoting mental well-being. Gardening, too, provides a therapeutic escape, connecting you with nature's rhythm. Digging in the soil, tending to plants, and watching them flourish can be a source of deep satisfaction and joy.

Reintegrating hobbies into your daily routine doesn't have to be overwhelming. The key is to set aside dedicated time each week for these activities. Give thought to blocking off an hour every Tuesday afternoon for your artistic endeavors or reserving Saturday mornings for tending your garden. By carving out this time, you create a ritual that becomes a cherished part of your routine. This consistency nurtures your interests and ensures that hobbies remain a priority amid life's demands. Over time, these moments become something to look forward to, a sanctuary where you can recharge and explore your creative side.

The social dimensions of hobbies should not be underestimated. Engaging in activities alongside others offers opportunities to meet like-minded individuals and build new friendships. Local clubs and community workshops serve as gathering places for those who share your passions. Whether it's a knitting circle that meets weekly or a photography group that organizes monthly outings, these settings foster connections that enrich your social life. Participating in classes or workshops provides a supportive environment to learn and grow. Here, you can exchange ideas, share techniques, and celebrate each other's progress. These interactions enhance the joy of hobbies, turning solitary pursuits into shared experiences.

Interactive Element: Hobby Exploration Checklist

Take a moment to reflect on hobbies that pique your interest or those you've always wanted to try. Create a checklist that includes these activities along with local clubs, workshops, or classes that offer them. Explore community centers or online resources to find opportunities that align with your interests. This checklist can guide you in planning your engagement with hobbies, ensuring they become an integral and enjoyable part of your retirement.

As you explore these hobbies, you may be drawn to new interests you hadn't considered before. The beauty of this stage in life is the freedom to experiment, to try something new without the pressure of perfection. Whether you choose to paint landscapes, tend a garden, or join a club, let these activities be a source of joy and fulfillment. Pursuing hobbies is a journey of discovery, one that invites you to engage with life in deeply rewarding ways.

5.1 LIFELONG LEARNING: EMBRACING EDUCATION AT ANY AGE

Picture yourself seated at your dining room table with a glass of iced tea as you dive into an online course. The world of lifelong learning is at your fingertips, offering boundless opportunities to expand your horizons. This stage of life, often seen as a time to slow down, can instead become a period of enrichment and growth. By embracing continuous education, you unlock personal development and fulfillment pathways that keep your mind agile and engaged. Visualize enrolling in courses from platforms like Coursera or Udemy, where you can explore everything from creative writing to data science. These platforms provide the flexibility to learn at your own pace, allowing you to delve into subjects that have always intrigued you. Whether you're deepening a long-held passion or venturing into new territories, the joy of learning lies in the discovery itself.

For those who prefer a more structured environment, local community colleges and adult education programs offer a wealth of resources. These institutions are treasure troves of knowledge waiting to be explored. Community colleges often provide courses tailored for retirees, making it easier to connect with peers who share your interests. Adult education classes cover a wide range of subjects, from languages to arts to technology, ensuring there's something for everyone. By attending these classes, you acquire new skills and become part of a community of learners, enriching your social life in unexpected ways. The camaraderie in these settings can be as rewarding as the knowledge gained, fostering friendships that enhance your educational experience.

The cognitive benefits of lifelong learning extend beyond the acquisition of new skills. Engaging in continuous education keeps your mind active and sharp, staving off cognitive decline associated with aging. Think about studying a new language using apps like Duolingo, making language learning accessible and enjoyable. These apps offer bite-sized lessons that fit seamlessly into your daily routine, turning spare moments into opportunities for growth. Engaging in puzzles and logic games further stimulates your brain, challenging you to think critically and solve problems. These activities provide mental exercise and instill a sense of accomplishment, boosting your confidence and sense of agency. You create a fusion of intellectual engagement that enriches your life with learning that enhancing your days.

Setting educational goals is a powerful way to focus your efforts and track your progress. These goals are steppingstones, guiding you toward your broader aspirations. Begin by identifying areas you wish to explore, then create a personalized learning plan with clear milestones. This plan serves as a roadmap, helping you stay organized and motivated. Whether you aim to complete a specific course, master a new skill, or indulge your curiosity, having defined objectives provides direction and purpose. Tracking your progress along the way allows you to celebrate achievements, no matter how small, reinforcing the joy of learning. By maintaining a sense of curiosity and openness, you invite endless opportunities for discovery and growth into your life.

5.2 ENCORE CAREERS: TURNING PASSION INTO PURPOSE

Imagine stepping into a role that aligns with your deepest passions and brings a profound sense of fulfillment. Encore careers offer this unique opportunity, allowing you to pursue work that resonates with your values and interests, even after stepping away from your primary career. These roles can take many forms, from consulting to teaching, and often provide a chance to leverage years of experience in new and meaningful ways. For instance, if you've spent decades in corporate management, you might find joy in mentoring young entrepreneurs or leading workshops that teach business fundamentals. Teaching, whether in a local community college or through online platforms, can also be an enriching avenue, allowing you to impart knowledge while staying engaged with a subject you love. The beauty of an encore career lies in its flexibility and purpose, enabling you to shape this new chapter of life around what truly matters to you.

Identifying a potential encore career begins with introspection. Reflect on your skills, interests, and what brings you joy. Study what aspects of your previous work you found most rewarding and how they might translate into a new career. Self-assessment exercises can be invaluable, helping you uncover strengths and passions you may not have fully recognized. For example, jot down your professional accomplishments and interests, then look for patterns or connections to guide your encore career choice.

Perhaps you've always had a knack for organizing events or a passion for writing. These insights can point you toward opportunities that align with your talents and desires, setting the stage for a fulfilling and purpose-driven career.

Pursuing an encore career offers numerous benefits that extend beyond financial stability. These roles can provide a renewed sense of purpose, helping you stay mentally and socially engaged. They also open doors to mentorship and leadership opportunities within your chosen field, allowing you to guide and support others while continuing your own professional growth. Envision the satisfaction of mentoring a group of aspiring professionals or leading a community project that makes a tangible difference. These experiences enrich your life and positively impact those around you. Furthermore, an encore career can bridge retirement and full-time work, offering the flexibility to balance work with leisure and other interests.

Transitioning into an encore career requires careful planning and a proactive approach. Start by building connections in your desired field through networking. Attend industry events, join professional associations, and engage with online communities to meet others who share your interests. Networking introduces you to potential opportunities and provides insights and advice from those already established in the field. Online resources can also be instrumental in facilitating career transitions. Websites like LinkedIn offer tools for career exploration and skill development. At the same time, platforms such as Coursera provide courses that can help you update or acquire new skills relevant to your chosen path. By leveraging these resources, you can equip yourself with the knowledge and connections needed to succeed in your encore career.

5.3 VOLUNTEERING WITH IMPACT: FINDING THE RIGHT FIT

Imagine finding a role that fills your days with purpose and leaves an indelible mark on the community around you. Purposeful volunteering provides this opportunity, bridging the gap between personal growth and community betterment. Choosing roles that resonate with your passions and skills allows you to contribute meaningfully while enriching your life. In local nonprofits, roles vary from mentoring young students in literacy programs to organizing events for community outreach. These positions provide a platform to apply your unique talents in ways that make a tangible difference. Engaging in such roles supports vital community needs and fosters a profound sense of fulfillment and accomplishment, inviting you to become an integral part of the community's fabric.

To find the right volunteering opportunity, consider what you enjoy and where your strengths lie. Reflect on past experiences that brought you joy or a sense of achievement. Perhaps you thrived in leadership roles or found satisfaction in creative endeavors. Once you have a clearer picture, explore volunteering databases like VolunteerMatch or Idealist. These platforms act as bridges, connecting you with causes that align with your interests. Whether it's working with animals, supporting environmental initiatives, or helping in educational settings, these resources simplify the process of finding the perfect fit. By specifying your preferences and skills, you're more likely to find an opportunity that feels rewarding and genuinely engaging. This approach ensures that your volunteer work benefits others and enhances your sense of purpose and satisfaction.

The benefits of volunteering extend beyond the immediate impact of your efforts. It creates an environment where personal fulfillment and community support go hand in hand. As you work alongside fellow volunteers, you forge relationships built on shared goals and camaraderie. These connections often blossom into friendships, providing a social network that enriches your life. Furthermore, volunteering allows you to gain new skills and insights, broadening your horizons and enhancing your adaptability. Whether learning event planning, developing communication skills, or acquiring practical knowledge in a new field, these experiences contribute to your personal growth. They equip you with valuable tools in volunteer settings that are applicable to various aspects of life. Through volunteering, you engage in a continuous cycle of learning and giving, each reinforcing the other.

Consistency is key to making a lasting impact through volunteer work. Regular involvement allows you to build deeper relationships within the organization and community, making your contributions more meaningful. Consider setting a volunteer schedule that suits your lifestyle, whether weekly, bi-weekly, or monthly commitments. This regularity benefits the organization by providing reliable support and seamlessly integrating volunteering into your routine. By committing to a consistent schedule, you reinforce your role as a dependable and valued member of the team. Over time, this commitment leads to more significant projects and responsibilities, amplifying your impact and deepening your connection to the cause. Regular volunteering becomes a rhythm that adds structure and purpose to your days, enriching your life and those you touch.

5.4 TRAVELING WITH A PURPOSE: COMBINING LEISURE AND SERVICE

Picture stepping off a plane in a new country, your senses alive with the colors, sounds, and scents of a place waiting to be explored. But this isn't just any trip—it's one where you combine leisure with meaningful service, creating a medley of experiences that enrich your life and those you meet. This is purposeful travel, a chance to immerse yourself in different cultures while contributing to the local community. Programs like Habitat for Humanity offer such opportunities, where you can help build homes and hope, connecting with people in ways that ordinary tourism often doesn't allow.

The appeal of purposeful travel lies in its ability to transform a vacation into a deeply enriching experience. Visualize spending a week in a small village, working alongside locals on community projects. You learn about their traditions, share meals, and engage in conversations that deepen your understanding of the world. This kind of travel fosters a genuine cultural exchange, breaking down barriers and building bridges. It allows you to step outside your comfort zone, embracing the unknown with curiosity and openness. Through these interactions, you gain insights that challenge preconceived notions, fostering empathy and broadening your worldview. Such experiences are transformative and leave a lasting impact on the communities you assist, creating memories that linger long after you've returned home.

Planning a purposeful trip requires some research and organization. Begin by exploring organizations like Global Volunteers, which offer structured programs designed to match your skills and interests with community needs. These organizations provide the framework and support necessary to ensure your efforts are practical and appreciated. They often handle logistics such as accommodation and meals, allowing you to focus on the work and the experience. Think about your abilities and what you hope to gain from the trip, then choose a program that aligns with these goals. Whether you're drawn to teaching English, participating in environmental conservation, or assisting in healthcare initiatives, there's a project that can benefit from your enthusiasm and expertise. These opportunities allow you to engage with the world in meaningful ways, enriching your travel experiences beyond what sightseeing alone can offer.

As you embark on these journeys, it's valuable to document your experiences, capturing the moments that resonate deeply with you. Keeping a travel log can be a powerful tool for reflection, helping you process and appreciate the impact of your trip. Write about the people you meet, the challenges you face, and the lessons you learn. These reflections enhance your personal growth and serve as a record of your contributions and the change you've witnessed. Photos and sketches can complement your words, adding a visual dimension to your memories. Upon returning home, revisiting these entries can provide clarity and perspective, reinforcing the personal growth and cultural understanding gained through your travels. Sharing your stories with friends and family can also inspire others to contemplate purposeful travel, spreading the message of global citizenship and service.

Purposeful travel invites you to see the world through a different lens, where every interaction holds the potential for learning and connection. It challenges you to engage with communities in a way that respects and honors their traditions while contributing positively to their development. This kind of travel offers a chance to give back, creating a ripple effect of goodwill and understanding that extends far beyond the boundaries of the trip itself. As you plan your next adventure, consider how you might incorporate service into your itinerary, transforming your travels into an enriching experience that benefits you and the world around you.

5.5 MENTORING: SHARING WISDOM AND BUILDING LEGACY

Imagine the profound impact of sharing your life's wisdom with someone eager to learn and grow. Mentoring offers this invaluable opportunity, allowing you to impart your knowledge and experiences to younger generations. In doing so, you help shape their futures while creating a legacy beyond your immediate circle. Programs within local schools or community centers provide structured avenues to engage in mentoring, offering a platform to guide and inspire. Whether it's mentoring a young student struggling with math or advising an aspiring entrepreneur on business strategies, these relationships have the power to transform lives. By sharing your journey, you enrich others and reinforce the value of your experiences.

To become an effective mentor, it's essential to cultivate specific skills that foster open and meaningful relationships. Active listening is at the heart of any successful mentoring relationship. It involves giving full attention, acknowledging feelings, and responding thoughtfully. This creates a safe space where mentees feel heard and valued, encouraging them to share their thoughts and challenges. Strong communication skills are equally important, ensuring that advice is conveyed clearly and constructively. By practicing empathy and patience, you can guide mentees through their difficulties, helping them find solutions and build confidence. These interactions also offer opportunities for personal growth as you learn from your mentees' perspectives and experiences.

The rewards of mentoring extend far beyond the satisfaction of helping others. Such relationships often foster a sense of achievement and fulfillment that enriches your life. Consider the pride in seeing your mentee succeed, knowing that your guidance played a role in their journey. These stories of successful mentoring relationships illustrate the profound impact that mentorship can have. Give thought to the case of a retired teacher who mentored a high school student, helping them gain confidence and improve their academic performance. This success benefited the student and gave the mentor a renewed sense of purpose and connection. As a mentor, you gain as much as you give, discovering new insights and rejuvenating your own enthusiasm for learning and growth.

Participating in formal mentoring programs can enhance your mentoring experience, providing support and resources to help you succeed. Local and online mentoring networks connect you with individuals seeking guidance in various fields. These programs often offer training sessions, workshops, and resources to help you develop your mentoring skills. By joining such initiatives, you become part of a community of mentors who share your commitment to making a difference. The possibilities are vast and varied, whether you choose a program focused on education, business, or personal development. Engaging in these networks expands your reach and enriches your mentoring experience with diverse perspectives and ideas.

As you consider the role of mentoring in your life, remember that it is a dynamic and evolving process. Each interaction offers the chance to learn and grow, both for you and your mentee. Through mentoring, you create a lasting legacy that touches lives and inspires future generations. Your wisdom becomes a guiding light, illuminating paths and opening doors for those who follow. In sharing your knowledge, you ensure that your impact endures, resonating long after your mentoring journey has concluded. This chapter on purposeful engagement and new opportunities underscores the myriad ways to enrich your life in retirement, from hobbies to mentoring. As you welcome these opportunities, you'll find that they enhance your days, filling them with meaningful interactions and lifelong learning.

6

NAVIGATING FAMILY DYNAMICS AND RELATIONSHIPS

I magine a Sunday afternoon at your home, the air filled with the aroma of freshly brewed coffee. Your daughter stops by with her kids, and suddenly, your quiet retreat transforms into a lively gathering. While these moments bring joy, they also highlight the need to balance family interactions with personal time. As women, we often wear many hats—caretaker, mediator, confidante—which is even more pronounced as we transition into retirement. The challenge lies in setting boundaries that honor our needs and our families. This chapter invites you to explore the art of boundary-setting to maintain harmony and personal well-being.

6.1 SETTING BOUNDARIES: BALANCING FAMILY NEEDS AND PERSONAL TIME

Setting boundaries can sometimes feel elusive, yet it is essential for maintaining healthy relationships and preserving our sense of self. Visualize boundaries as invisible lines that define where your responsibilities end, and others begin. These lines protect your time, energy, and emotional resources, ensuring you can nurture yourself while being present for your family. Clear boundaries help manage expectations, allowing family members to understand your limits and respect your space. They prevent overextension and resentment, creating a foundation for mutual respect and understanding.

Assertive communication is key to establishing these boundaries effectively. It involves expressing your needs clearly and confidently, without anger or guilt. Techniques like using "I" statements can be helpful. For example, saying, "I need some quiet time in the afternoons to recharge," communicates your needs without placing blame. Creating a family calendar can also be a practical tool to allocate time for personal and family activities. By visibly scheduling commitments and downtime, you set expectations and reduce the chances of overbooking. This visual representation is a gentle reminder to you and your family to honor the time set aside for yourself.

Maintaining boundaries requires strategies that uphold your decisions without guilt or discomfort. One approach is to practice saying no gracefully. It's okay to decline requests that encroach on your personal time. Phrases like, "I appreciate the invitation, but I need some time to myself," can convey your decision kindly yet firmly. It's important to remember that saying no to others often means saying yes to yourself, opening up space for activities that rejuvenate you. Upholding boundaries might feel challenging initially, but over time, it becomes a liberating practice that empowers you to lead a balanced life.

Open dialogue about needs and limits is crucial in fostering understanding and cooperation within your family. Regular family meetings provide a platform to discuss boundaries and adjust them as necessary. During these meetings, encourage each member to express their needs and listen actively to others. This open communication nurtures empathy and creates an environment where everyone's boundaries are respected. It also offers an opportunity to address any concerns or conflicts that may arise, ensuring that solutions are collaborative and considerate.

Examine common scenarios where setting boundaries is necessary, such as handling requests for childcare or errands. While it can be rewarding to support your family, it's essential to be mindful of your capacity. If a family member frequently asks for help, you might say, "I'm happy to assist occasionally, but I also need time for my own activities." This statement acknowledges your willingness to help while clearly defining your limits. By setting these boundaries, you preserve your energy and maintain balance in your life.

Interactive Element: Boundary-Setting Reflection

Reflect on a recent instance when you felt your personal boundaries were being encroached upon. Consider your reaction to this situation and how alternative communication might have protected your boundaries better. Jot down some "I" statements or alternative responses that would have more clearly expressed your needs. This reflective exercise is designed to enhance your assertive communication skills, equipping you for future situations that may require firm boundary-setting.

Navigating family dynamics in retirement offers challenges and opportunities for growth. By setting and maintaining clear boundaries, you create a harmonious environment that respects your and your family's needs, allowing you to enjoy your relationships while nurturing your well-being.

6.2 PARTNERING IN RETIREMENT: STRENGTHENING MARITAL BONDS

Retirement brings a significant shift in marital dynamics, transforming the daily rhythm couples have known for years. With career obligations behind you, the time spent together often increases, necessitating adjustments in how roles are shared. This phase can be rewarding and challenging, as it invites reevaluating household responsibilities. Picture a typical day where both of you share chores with ease, whether it's preparing meals or organizing the home. This mutual participation fosters a sense of equality and partnership, creating a balanced environment where both partners feel valued and supported. By sharing these tasks, you lighten the load and cultivate a deeper connection through teamwork and cooperation.

Beyond the practicalities of daily life, retirement offers a unique opportunity to strengthen the intimacy and connection that underpin a lasting marriage. Planning regular date nights or joint activities can rekindle the spark, reminding you of the joy found in each other's company. Whether it's a cozy dinner at home, a walk in the park, or a weekend getaway, these shared experiences build memories that enrich your bond. Additionally, practicing active listening and empathy provides a foundation for understanding and closeness. This involves truly hearing each other, acknowledging feelings, and responding with compassion. Creating a safe space for open dialogue nurtures a relationship where both partners feel heard and cherished.

Shared goals and activities are vital in enhancing marital satisfaction during retirement. Pursuing common interests fosters a sense of purpose and unity, turning shared dreams into reality. Think about taking up a new hobby together, such as gardening, painting, or learning a musical instrument. These ventures offer opportunities to grow and discover new aspects of each other, keeping your relationship vibrant and dynamic. Planning travel adventures can also bring excitement and anticipation as you explore new destinations and cultures. These shared endeavors strengthen your bond and create a melting pot of experiences that enrich your lives.

Resolving conflicts constructively is crucial for maintaining harmony, especially when spending more time together. Effective communication is key and using "I" statements can be a powerful tool. For example, expressing, "I feel overwhelmed when the house is cluttered," rather than assigning blame, opens the door for collaboration and problem-solving. This approach encourages both partners to take responsibility for their feelings and actions, fostering a sense of partnership in addressing issues. It's about finding solutions that respect both perspectives, ensuring that disagreements become opportunities for growth rather than sources of tension. By addressing conflicts with kindness and understanding, you create a resilient and harmonious relationship that thrives in the face of change.

Retirement is a chapter that invites reflection and renewal, offering couples the chance to deepen their connection and envision new possibilities. By adopting these strategies, you can navigate the shifts in marital dynamics with grace and joy, ensuring that your partnership remains a source of strength and fulfillment. The journey may require adjustments, but with open hearts and minds, it promises to be a rewarding experience.

6.3 GRANDPARENTING: JOYS AND CHALLENGES IN A NEW ROLE

The role of grandparenting often arrives with a wave of joy, introducing new dimensions to family life. Grandchildren's laughter fills your home, creating a warm, lively, invigorating, and comforting atmosphere. There's a unique kind of fulfillment in this stage, where you can engage with your grandchildren without the pressures of being a parent. You have the opportunity to create memorable traditions, such as baking cookies every Sunday or embarking on nature walks to discover the wonders of the outdoors together. These activities foster deep bonds and pass down values and stories that shape the young ones' understanding of their heritage and identity.

Yet, grandparenting is not without its challenges. Balancing your involvement with personal time can be a delicate act, especially when you cherish your newfound freedom in retirement. The excitement of spending time with grandchildren can sometimes lead to overcommitment, leaving you stretched thin. Managing expectations becomes crucial, as family members may assume your availability for babysitting or other tasks. It's essential to clearly communicate your limits, ensuring your time and energy are protected. This balance allows you to enjoy precious moments with your grandchildren while maintaining the space you need for yourself.

Building strong relationships with your grandchildren involves more than just spending time together; it requires intentional interaction. Sharing family stories or history can be an enriching experience, offering children a sense of belonging and continuity. These tales become a bridge between generations, connecting your past with their present. Engaging in educational or creative activities, such as crafting or reading together, can also strengthen these bonds. These shared experiences nurture curiosity, learning, and create a reservoir of cherished memories they will carry into adulthood.

As a grandparent, setting boundaries around your personal space while enjoying your role is essential for maintaining balance. Establishing regular visitation schedules can help manage your needs and those of your family. This approach ensures that you can plan activities around your commitments while still being an integral part of your grandchildren's lives. It's about finding the sweet spot where you can be present and supportive without feeling overwhelmed. By setting these parameters, you create a healthy dynamic that respects your autonomy and fosters a nurturing environment for your grandchildren.

Grandparenting is a journey filled with love, laughter, and growth. It offers you the chance to impact your grandchildren's lives positively while continuing to learn and adapt. Welcome this role with an open heart, allowing yourself the freedom to explore the joys and navigate the challenges with confidence and grace.

6.4 THE SANDWICH GENERATION: CARING FOR PARENTS AND CHILDREN

Suppose you're juggling a conference call while preparing dinner, and just as you're about to catch a breath, your phone buzzes with a message from your mom about her latest medical appointment. This scene encapsulates the life of many in the sandwich generation, caught between the needs of aging parents and adult children. It's a delicate balance, requiring emotional resilience and logistical prowess. Caring for elderly parents often involves coordinating care plans, managing medications, and attending numerous appointments. It's a role that demands patience, compassion, and the ability to navigate healthcare systems and advocate for your parent's needs. At the same time, your adult children may need support, whether a listening ear or help with their parenting challenges. Balancing these dual responsibilities can feel overwhelming, as each day presents a new set of priorities and demands.

To manage these caregiving roles effectively, setting clear priorities is crucial. Begin by identifying which duties are most urgent and which can wait. This might mean addressing a parent's immediate health concern before helping a child with a routine matter. Once priorities are established, review delegating tasks when possible. Enlist the help of siblings or other family members to share the load. If you're managing a parent's medical appointments, perhaps a sibling can assist with grocery shopping or household chores. Community resources and support groups can also provide assistance and relief. Many organizations offer caregiver support programs, providing respite care and counseling services. These resources can be invaluable, offering a network of support and expertise to help you navigate the complexities of caregiving.

Amid these responsibilities, it's vital to prioritize your own well-being. As caregivers, we often place our needs last, but neglecting self-care can lead to burnout and fatigue. Schedule regular activities that rejuvenate you, whether a brisk walk, a yoga class, or simply reading a book. These moments of self-care are not selfish —they're necessary for maintaining your physical and mental health. Taking care of yourself ensures you have the energy and resilience to support your family effectively. Remember, you can't pour from an empty cup, so make self-care a non-negotiable part of your routine.

Effective communication is key to managing caregiving roles and responsibilities. Family meetings provide a platform to discuss duties and share updates on your parent's health and well-being. During these gatherings, encourage open dialogue to ensure everyone is on the same page. Discuss the challenges you're facing and explore solutions collaboratively. By working together, family members can devise a plan that distributes tasks equitably and respects each person's capacity. If tensions arise, approach them with empathy and a willingness to understand different perspectives. By fostering an environment of cooperation and understanding, you create a support system that benefits everyone involved.

Caring for parents and children is no small feat, but with the right strategies and support, it can be a fulfilling aspect of your life. Accept this role with compassion and determination, knowing that your efforts make a significant difference in the lives of those you love. As you navigate the challenges of the sandwich generation, take pride in the strength and resilience you demonstrate each day.

6.5 COMMUNICATING EFFECTIVELY WITH FAMILY MEMBERS

We all know that communication is the glue that holds a family together. It's not just about exchanging words; it's about fostering understanding and cooperation among the people we love. Envision trying to assemble a puzzle without all the pieces fitting together—communication fills those gaps. Practicing active listening is one way to enhance this vital skill. When we truly listen, we give our full attention to the person speaking, setting aside distractions and judgments. This simple act can transform interactions, making others feel valued and understood. In a world full of noise, being genuinely heard is a gift.

Improving communication within the family involves more than just listening; it requires clarity and simplicity in how we express ourselves. Using clear and concise language avoids misunderstandings and minimizes assumptions. Think of it as painting with bold strokes instead of intricate details—direct yet gentle. Also, encouraging open-ended questions invites dialogue and exploration rather than shutting down conversations. Questions like, "What do you think about this idea?" or "How do you feel about the changes happening?" open the floor for discussions, inviting everyone to share their thoughts and feelings openly. This approach enriches conversations and strengthens bonds by promoting understanding.

Family conflicts are inevitable, but how we handle them can make all the difference. Conflict resolution techniques offer pathways to peaceful outcomes, turning disagreements into opportunities for growth. Consider mediation or facilitated family discussions as tools to navigate these challenging waters. These structured conversations provide a safe space for everyone to voice their concerns, fostering an environment of mutual respect. By focusing on solutions rather than blame, families can work collaboratively to resolve issues. This process involves acknowledging each person's perspective, validating their feelings, and seeking common ground. It's about building bridges, not walls, and finding ways to move forward together.

Regular family check-ins are an excellent way to address concerns and share updates, ensuring everyone remains connected and informed. Setting aside time for weekly or monthly family meetings creates a routine that supports open communication and transparency. These gatherings offer a platform to discuss any changes, challenges, or achievements, keeping everyone on the same page. By maintaining this rhythm of communication, families can prevent misunderstandings and strengthen their connections. It's also an opportunity to celebrate successes, no matter how small, fostering a sense of unity and shared purpose.

In the tapestry of family life, communication is the thread that weaves through every interaction, binding us together in a shared narrative. By embracing these techniques and practices, you can cultivate a family environment that thrives on understanding, compassion, and cooperation. Effective communication empowers each member to express themselves authentically, enriching relationships and creating a harmonious home.

6.6 INVOLVING FAMILY IN YOUR RETIREMENT JOURNEY

Retirement, a time often marked by personal reflection and new beginnings, can also offer an excellent opportunity to strengthen your family ties. Sharing your retirement goals with your family is more than just a conversation—it's an invitation for them to understand and support you as you transition into this new phase of life. By discussing your financial plans, you provide clarity and foster a sense of inclusion, ensuring everyone is on the same page. Imagine sitting with your loved ones around the dining table, openly sharing your aspirations, whether it's downsizing to a cozy home or embarking on that long-dreamed-of cross-country road trip. These discussions build mutual understanding and allow family members to offer their insights and perhaps even join you in some of your adventures. When family members know your plans, they can become allies in helping you achieve them, offering advice or assistance where needed, and celebrating milestones as they occur.

Involving your family in retirement experiences can deepen these connections. Contemplate inviting them to participate in volunteer projects that align with your values and interests. Whether it's planting trees in a local park or helping at the community food bank, these shared activities foster a sense of purpose and strengthen familial bonds. Volunteering together enriches your retirement and sets an example of service and community engagement for younger family members. Hosting family events or gatherings also provides a chance to connect. From casual backyard barbecues to more structured family reunions, these occasions allow you to share your retirement journey in a quiet setting. Such gatherings provide a platform for storytelling, laughter, and the creation of new memories, reinforcing the ties that bind your family together.

Managing family expectations is crucial to maintaining harmony during your retirement. Setting realistic boundaries and roles within joint activities or projects is important. For instance, if you're spearheading a family reunion, clearly define who will handle logistics, manage invitations, and coordinate activities. This clarity prevents misunderstandings and ensures that everyone feels valued and involved. Family members are more likely to embrace their responsibilities and contribute positively when roles are well-defined. Setting these expectations from the outset creates a collaborative environment where everyone knows their part and works together toward a common goal.

Celebrating milestones with your family can bring immense joy and a sense of accomplishment. Whether it's your retirement anniversary or the completion of a significant personal project, these moments are worth acknowledging. Planning joint celebrations for such achievements allows you to share your triumphs with those you love. You might host a dinner to toast a year of retirement or organize a small gathering to unveil a creative project you've completed. These celebrations highlight your successes and provide an opportunity for your family to express their pride and support. They reinforce the idea that retirement is a vibrant time of life, filled with achievements and new adventures, and that your family is an integral part of that journey.

Through these shared experiences, you create a rich medley of family connections that enhance your retirement. Involving your family in your plans, activities, and celebrations fosters a supportive and collaborative environment that enriches your life and theirs. As you move forward, these bonds will continue to grow, offering comfort, joy, and a sense of belonging. Retirement becomes not just an individual experience, but a shared one filled with love, laughter, and lasting memories.

7

MAINTAINING PHYSICAL AND MENTAL WELLNESS

Visualize standing at the edge of a serene lake, early morning mist swirling around you, the air crisp and invigorating. This scene embodies the essence of retirement—a time to refresh and renew, to welcome the vitality that comes from nurturing body and mind. In this stage of life, maintaining physical and mental wellness becomes not just a goal but a necessity for a vibrant and fulfilling existence. As we explore ways to stay active, remember that each movement you make is a step towards longevity and enhanced quality of life.

7.1 STAYING ACTIVE: EXERCISE ROUTINES FOR EVERY LEVEL

Regular physical activity is your ally in the quest for a long, healthy life. Exercise is more than just movement; it's a powerful tool that supports cardiovascular health, strengthens bones, and boosts mood. Engaging in regular exercise can reduce the risk of chronic illnesses, such as heart disease and diabetes, and enhance cognitive function, giving you the energy and mental clarity to savor each day fully. The benefits extend beyond the physical, as exercise also acts as a balm for the psyche, releasing endorphins that uplift the spirit and foster a sense of achievement.

Incorporating a variety of exercise routines into your life can cater to different fitness levels and preferences, ensuring that staying active remains enjoyable and sustainable. For those seeking gentle pursuit, low-impact exercises like walking and swimming offer an ideal starting point. Walking, a simple yet effective exercise, strengthens muscles and lowers the risk of several diseases. On the other hand, swimming provides a full-body workout, engaging multiple muscle groups without placing undue stress on the joints. These activities can be easily adapted to your pace, gradually allowing you to build endurance and strength.

Strength training, an often-overlooked aspect of fitness, plays a crucial role in maintaining muscle mass and bone density as we age. Incorporating exercises like light weightlifting or resistance band workouts can help preserve physical functionality, enabling you to perform daily tasks with ease and confidence. These routines can be tailored to suit your comfort level, gradually increasing intensity as your strength improves. Strength training sessions can be done at home with minimal equipment, making them accessible and convenient.

To make physical activity a seamless part of daily life, give thought to integrating movement into routine tasks. Household chores, such as gardening or cleaning, can double as exercise, providing a practical way to stay active without dedicating extra time. Gardening, in particular, offers a unique combination of physical exertion and mental relaxation. Planting, weeding, and harvesting burn calories and foster a connection with nature, providing a sense of peace and accomplishment. These activities transform mundane tasks into opportunities for movement, keeping you engaged and active throughout the day.

Participating in group exercise classes or local walking clubs can provide additional motivation and enjoyment. The social aspect of group activities creates a supportive environment, encouraging you to push beyond perceived limits while fostering camaraderie and friendship. Joining a dance class or community yoga group offers a chance to learn new skills and meet like-minded individuals, enhancing physical and emotional well-being. These gatherings provide a sense of belonging and shared purpose, reminding you that the journey to wellness is one best traveled together.

Interactive Element: Craft Your Fitness Schedule

Take a moment to design a weekly fitness schedule that incorporates a mix of exercises you enjoy. Include at least two low-impact activities like walking or swimming sessions and add strength training exercises twice a week. Contemplate joining a local group class for social interaction. Track your progress over the next month, noting how you feel physically and mentally. This schedule serves as a guide to ensure that physical activity remains a consistent and rewarding part of your routine.

7.2 NUTRITION AND WELLNESS: EATING FOR LONGEVITY

Envision a kitchen bathed in sunlight, brimming with the vibrant colors of fresh fruits and vegetables. Every color signifies the variety of nutrients within, each serving as a cornerstone for sustained health and longevity. The role of nutrition is fundamental, underpinning our physical and mental well-being. A balanced diet lays the groundwork for optimal health, fueling our bodies to function at their peak. Eating goes beyond mere satiety; it involves enriching our bodies with a diverse array of nutrients that collectively bolster our health.

Consuming a wide range of nutrients is crucial. Think of your diet as a mosaic, each piece representing a different group: carbohydrates, fats, proteins, vitamins, and minerals. Together, they form a complete picture of health. Including a variety of fruits and vegetables in your meals ensures you receive an array of vitamins and antioxidants, which help fend off illness and keep you feeling vibrant. Lean proteins, like chicken, fish, and legumes, play a vital role in repairing tissues and building muscle, while whole grains provide sustained energy and support heart health. This balance helps maintain a healthy weight, reducing the risk of chronic diseases that can diminish your quality of life.

Guidelines for a balanced diet are simple yet impactful. Aim to fill half your plate with fruits and vegetables at each meal. This practice adds color and flavor to your dishes but also boosts your intake of essential nutrients. Incorporate lean proteins and whole grains into your meals, focusing on portion sizes that satisfy without overindulging. These foods support your body's needs, providing the energy required for daily activities and the nutrients necessary for overall health. By being mindful of what you eat, you set the stage for a vibrant lifestyle that supports your goals and aspirations.

Mindful eating transforms meals from a routine task into a meaningful experience. It encourages you to savor each bite, paying attention to flavors, textures, and aromas. This practice helps you recognize hunger cues, allowing you to eat in response to your body's needs rather than external triggers. Begin by taking a moment to appreciate your food before you eat. Chew slowly, noticing the taste and texture of each mouthful. This awareness enhances enjoyment but also aids digestion and prevents overeating. By cultivating a mindful approach to eating, you create a positive relationship with food that nourishes body and mind.

Hydration is a foundation of health, yet it's often overlooked. Water is essential for every cell and function in your body, from regulating temperature to transporting nutrients. Aim to drink at least eight glasses of water daily, more if you're active or in a hot climate. Listen to your body; thirst is a clear signal that you need to hydrate, but don't wait until you're parched to take a sip. Signs of dehydration can include fatigue, dizziness, and dry skin. Keeping a water bottle nearby can serve as a reminder to drink regularly throughout the day, ensuring your body remains well-hydrated and ready to tackle whatever comes your way.

7.3 MINDFULNESS AND MEDITATION: TOOLS FOR EMOTIONAL HEALTH

Picture settling into a comfy chair as the day's chaos gently fades away, replaced by a soothing sense of tranquility. This is the power of mindfulness and meditation, practices nurturing emotional well-being for centuries. In our fast-paced lives, these simple yet profound techniques offer a refuge—a way to center ourselves in the present moment. Practicing mindfulness means paying attention to the here and now and observing your thoughts and feelings without judgment. This awareness helps reduce anxiety and stress, creating a space where peace can flourish. Meditation, a close companion to mindfulness, deepens this experience by focusing your mind, often through a specific technique or mantra. Together, they form a powerful duo, fostering resilience and emotional balance.

Bringing meditation into your daily routine doesn't require hours of dedication or a unique setting. Start with brief guided breathing exercises, which can be done anywhere, anytime. Find a comfortable spot, close your eyes, and take a deep breath in through your nose, letting your chest and abdomen expand. Hold it for a moment, then exhale slowly through your mouth. Repeat this process, allowing each breath to wash away tension and invite tranquility. This simple practice quiets your body and quiets your mind, bringing clarity and focus to your day. Another effective technique is the body scan meditation, which promotes awareness by focusing on different parts of your body in sequence. Begin at your toes and gradually move upward, pausing to notice any sensations or tension. This practice helps ground you in the present, fostering a deeper connection between mind and body.

Establishing a regular meditation routine can be a transformative commitment to your well-being. Designate a specific time each day for your practice, whether it's a few peaceful minutes in the morning or a calming session before bed. Creating a dedicated space for meditation, free from distractions, enhances the experience. This could be a quiet place in your home where you can retreat, surrounded by objects that bring you peace, such as a soft cushion or a gentle candle. Consistency is key; even a short, daily practice can yield significant benefits over time. As you cultivate this habit, your ability to manage stress and navigate life's challenges strengthens, bringing a newfound sense of balance and contentment.

The accessibility of mindfulness resources makes it easier than ever to integrate these practices into your life. Technology offers a wealth of tools, from apps to online courses, that guide you through meditation exercises. Apps like Headspace and Calm provide a library of guided sessions catering to beginners and seasoned practitioners. These apps offer various meditation techniques, from quick breathing exercises to longer, more immersive experiences. They also include features like sleep stories, nature sounds, and daily reminders, supporting your practice and encouraging regular engagement. With these resources, you can tailor your mindfulness journey to fit your lifestyle, ensuring that peace and presence are always within reach.

7.4 BRAIN FITNESS: KEEPING YOUR MIND SHARP

Assume your brain as a garden, flourishing with vibrant thoughts and ideas. Keeping this garden thriving requires regular tending, and that's where brain fitness comes into play. Engaging your mind is crucial for maintaining sharpness and mental acuity. As we age, it's natural for cognitive function to shift, but the good news is that there are countless activities to help keep your mind agile and resilient. Cognitive exercises are a great starting point. They enhance memory and concentration, much like how daily watering and sunlight support the growth of a garden. Solving puzzles, such as crosswords or Sudoku, can be challenging and satisfying, offering a mental workout that strengthens neural connections. These activities require focus and strategy, pushing your brain to think in new ways.

In addition to puzzles, reflect on the benefits of playing strategic games. Chess, for instance, is a classic game that tests your ability to plan ahead and anticipate your opponent's moves. If chess seems daunting, card games like bridge or even digital strategy games can provide similar cognitive stimulation. These games encourage problem-solving and critical thinking, keeping your mind nimble and engaged. For a different challenge, learning a new language or musical instrument offers a double benefit: you acquire a new skill and give your brain a comprehensive workout. Language learning involves memorization and understanding complex grammar while playing an instrument requires coordination and timing. These activities stimulate different areas of the brain, promoting overall cognitive health and offering a sense of accomplishment.

Lifelong learning plays a pivotal role in brain fitness, and the options are virtually limitless. Engaging in continued education keeps your mind active, whether through enrolling in workshops, attending lectures, or taking online courses. The process of learning something new is invigorating, sparking curiosity and enthusiasm. Perhaps you've always wanted to delve into a subject like art history or astronomy—now is the perfect time. These educational pursuits provide structure and purpose, expanding your knowledge and opening doors to new interests and communities. With the rise of digital learning platforms, you can easily access courses from top universities around the world, all from the comfort of your home. This global classroom offers a wealth of opportunities to explore topics that pique your interest and keep your brain active.

Social engagement is another powerful tool for maintaining cognitive health. Interacting with others stimulates brain function and fosters a sense of connection and belonging. Participating in group discussions or clubs can be particularly beneficial. Book clubs, for example, offer a chance to dive into literature and engage in thought-provoking conversations with fellow readers. These discussions challenge your perceptions and encourage you to consider diverse perspectives. Joining a debate club or a philosophy group provides an intellectual arena where ideas are exchanged and challenged, promoting critical thinking and mental agility. The social aspect of these interactions cannot be overstated; the camaraderie and exchange of ideas invigorate the mind, creating a dynamic environment for cognitive growth.

For those looking to combine physical and mental activities, ponder joining a dance class or a tai chi group. These activities require coordination and memorization, engaging body and mind in a harmonious dance. Not only do they provide physical benefits, but they also encourage social interaction and mental focus. The rhythm of movement and the joy of learning new steps offer a holistic approach to wellness, nurturing cognitive and physical health. In this way, brain fitness becomes a multifaceted endeavor, enriching your life with knowledge, creativity, and connection. Through these diverse activities, you cultivate a garden of mental well-being, ensuring that your mind remains vibrant and resilient throughout the years.

7.5 STRESS REDUCTION TECHNIQUES FOR A PEACEFUL LIFE

Picture a tightrope stretched across two buildings, the sky a vast expanse above, and the bustling city below. Walking this line of balance can feel much like managing the stress of daily life. Chronic stress is no small adversary; it weaves itself into our physical and mental well-being, impacting everything from cardiovascular health to emotional stability. When stress takes hold, it can cause your heart to race and your blood pressure to rise, straining your cardiovascular system and increasing the risk of heart disease. The body's natural response to stress, known as the fight-or-flight reaction, floods your system with adrenaline. While this can be helpful in short bursts, prolonged exposure can lead to fatigue, anxiety, and even depression.

Think about incorporating practical stress reduction techniques into your daily life to step back from this precipice. One effective method is progressive muscle relaxation. This involves tensing and then slowly releasing each muscle group, starting from your toes and working your way up to your head. The act of focusing on each muscle, in turn, can distract your mind from stressors, promoting a sense of serenity and restfulness. As you release tension, your body sends signals to your brain that it's time to relax, which can help lower your heart rate and blood pressure. This simple yet powerful exercise can be done in just a few minutes, offering a respite whenever stress begins to build.

Journaling is another valuable tool for processing emotions and managing stress. Think of it as a conversation with yourself, a space where you can pour out your thoughts without judgment. Writing about your worries and frustrations allows you to externalize them, making them feel more manageable. As you write, you may discover patterns in your thoughts or solutions that were previously obscured. Journaling also provides an opportunity to reflect on positive experiences and express gratitude, shifting your focus away from stressors and fostering a more balanced perspective. Whether you prefer to jot down a few lines each day or pen longer entries when needed, the act of writing can bring clarity and relief.

Incorporating tranquility into your daily routine doesn't require grand gestures. It's about finding small pockets of time when you can retreat and recharge. Schedule regular "me-time" for activities that bring you joy and peace, whether it's a warm bath, a quiet moment with a book, prayer, or simply sitting in silence. Examine these intervals as essential as any other appointment, allowing yourself to step away from the pressures of the day. By making relaxation a priority, you create a buffer against stress, equipping yourself to handle challenges with greater ease and resilience.

Hobbies play a pivotal role in stress management, providing a creative outlet and a form of escapism. Engaging in activities that you enjoy can significantly reduce stress levels. Whether it's painting, crafting, or gardening, these pursuits demand focus and engagement, drawing your attention away from stressors and immersing you in the present moment. Creative outlets activate the right hemisphere of the brain, responsible for imagination and intuition, fostering a sense of play and exploration. This shift from analytical thinking to creative expression can alleviate stress, offering a refreshing perspective on life's challenges. As you immerse yourself in the colors of a canvas or the textures of fabric, you find a sanctuary where stress cannot easily intrude.

Creating a stress-reduction plan is a proactive step toward cultivating peace in your life. Give thought to setting aside time each day for the activities that calm and center you. Reflect on what brings you joy and balance, and make these practices a regular part of your routine. Allow yourself the freedom to experiment with different techniques, discovering what resonates with you. As you integrate these practices into your life, you'll likely find that the tightrope of stress becomes less daunting, replaced by a path that feels steady and sure.

7.6 EMBRACING A HOLISTIC APPROACH TO WELL-BEING

Imagine your well-being as a beautifully intertwined tapestry, where each thread represents a different aspect of your life—physical, mental, and emotional. This interconnectedness forms the foundation of holistic health, which emphasizes the integration of body, mind, and spirit. By nurturing these elements collectively, you create a harmonious balance that supports overall wellness. A holistic approach recognizes that proper health extends beyond the absence of illness, aiming instead for a dynamic state where every part of your being thrives. It's about understanding how your emotions influence your physical state, how mental clarity can enhance your emotional resilience, and how spiritual practices can ground and center you.

Adopting a holistic lifestyle invites you to incorporate practices that honor this interconnectedness. Yoga and tai chi are excellent examples, offering gentle yet powerful ways to achieve physical and mental balance. These practices focus on breath control, flexibility, and mindful movement, fostering a deep connection between your body and mind. As you move through each pose or sequence, you cultivate awareness and inner peace, releasing tension and promoting vitality. Similarly, exploring alternative therapies like acupuncture or aromatherapy can enhance your holistic journey. Acupuncture, with its roots in traditional Chinese medicine, aims to restore energy flow and balance within the body. Aromatherapy, meanwhile, uses essential oils to uplift mood, reduce stress, and support emotional healing. By incorporating these practices into your routine, you create a holistic environment that nurtures every aspect of your well-being.

Self-awareness is a mainstay of holistic health, empowering you to understand and meet your personal needs. This awareness requires introspection and reflection, allowing you to identify areas of imbalance or distress. Techniques such as prayer or meditation can guide you in this exploration, providing clarity and insight. Journaling offers a space to articulate thoughts and emotions, uncovering patterns and triggers that may impact your well-being. Meditation invites stillness and presence, encouraging you to listen to your inner voice and align your actions with your true self. By engaging in these reflective practices, you develop a deeper connection to your needs and desires, fostering a sense of empowerment and self-compassion.

A commitment to holistic wellness is an ongoing journey, one that requires regular attention and adjustment. Just as you might schedule a health check-up, consider conducting regular check-ins with yourself to monitor and adjust your wellness practices. These moments of reflection allow you to assess what is working, what needs tweaking, and where you might introduce new elements to enhance your well-being. Perhaps you've noticed that daily meditation has brought increased peacefulness or that a particular yoga class invigorates your spirit. Celebrate these successes and remain open to exploring new avenues when needed. Remember, holistic wellness is not a destination but a continuous process that evolves with you, adapting to your changing needs and circumstances.

By embracing a holistic approach, you cultivate a rich, balanced, and fulfilling life. This perspective invites you to view health as a dynamic interplay between all facets of your being, encouraging growth and transformation. As you weave these practices into your daily life, you build a resilient foundation that supports your well-being, nurturing body and soul. Each choice you make reflects a commitment to living with intention and vitality, creating a blend of wellness that enhances every aspect of your existence.

8

EMBRACING TECHNOLOGY AND INNOVATION

R emember the first time you rode a bicycle. At first, it seemed daunting, perhaps even intimidating. But with each pedal, you grew more confident until the ride felt like second nature. In today's digital age, technology can feel just as intimidating, yet it holds the potential to enrich our lives in countless ways. Embracing technology during retirement opens doors to new experiences, connections, and conveniences. Technology is a powerful tool, whether it's keeping in touch with family, exploring hobbies, or managing daily tasks. Yet, like that first bicycle ride, it requires a bit of patience and practice to master.

8.1 BECOMING A SILVER SURFER: TECHNOLOGY BASICS FOR BEGINNERS

Let's start by demystifying the world of smartphones and tablets. Much like our old address books or photo albums, these devices have become essential companions in our daily lives. A simple swipe or tap allows you to connect with loved ones, capture precious moments, and explore new ideas. Navigating these devices begins with understanding the basic gestures: swiping to move through screens, pinching to zoom in and out, and tapping to select items. As you grow more comfortable, you'll discover a wealth of apps designed to simplify tasks and entertain. For those just beginning their journey with these devices, review exploring the settings menu, where you can adjust font sizes for easier reading or enable voice commands to assist with hands-free operation.

Moving on to computers, understanding standard software can be a game-changer. Programs like Microsoft Word or Google Docs allow you to write letters, create to-do lists, and even share documents with friends or family across the globe. These platforms often include templates that simplify tasks, from crafting a holiday newsletter to organizing a volunteer event. Learning to navigate these programs involves recognizing icons and understanding basic functions like saving, printing, and formatting text. Don't hesitate to explore the help sections or tutorials that many software programs offer, as they provide step-by-step guidance tailored to beginners.

Setting up and using an email account is another essential skill, akin to opening a virtual post office box. Email allows you to send and receive messages instantly, whether you're sharing a quick note with a friend or receiving essential updates from a community group. Begin by choosing a provider like Gmail or Yahoo, which offers user-friendly interfaces. The setup process typically involves creating a unique username and password, followed by a few security questions to protect your account. Once set up, familiarize yourself with composing emails, attaching files, and organizing your inbox using folders or labels. As you grow confident, you'll find that email becomes a vital tool for staying connected and informed.

Internet browsing is much like flipping through the pages of a vast library, each click opening new worlds of information. Start by selecting a web browser, such as Chrome, Edge, or Firefox, and practice entering web addresses or using search engines to find information. As you browse, you'll encounter hyperlinks—underlined words or phrases that, when clicked, transport you to related content. Understanding how to navigate forward and backward through pages, bookmark favorite sites, and recognize secure websites is key. Always be cautious about entering personal information and ensure that you are on trusted sites before making purchases or sharing sensitive details.

Feeling apprehensive about technology is natural, especially when faced with unfamiliar devices or software. Overcoming this anxiety begins with approaching technology as a learning opportunity rather than a challenge. Start by exploring troubleshooting strategies, such as restarting your device if it isn't working correctly or consulting online forums for solutions. Reflect on enrolling in tech workshops specifically designed for seniors, where you can learn in a supportive environment. Programs like Cyber-Seniors, which connect older adults with tech-savvy volunteers, offer free workshops and one-on-one assistance to help you gain confidence and skills.

For those eager to delve deeper, numerous resources can guide you in expanding your digital literacy. Free online tutorials and community classes, often available through local libraries or senior centers, provide structured learning opportunities. Websites like Senior Planet offer courses on a range of topics, from using social media to managing digital photos. These resources cater to various skill levels, allowing you to progress at your own pace. Whether you're mastering the basics or exploring advanced topics, the key is to remain curious and open to the possibilities that technology offers.

8.2 APPS FOR HEALTH AND WELLNESS: YOUR DIGITAL COACH

In the realm of personal wellness, technology has become a valuable ally, offering a range of apps designed to support physical, mental, and emotional health. Visualize having a personal trainer, nutritionist, and meditation guru all tucked into a device that fits in your pocket. This is the promise of health and wellness apps, which empower you to take control of your well-being with just a few taps. Fitness tracking apps like Fitbit or MyFitnessPal act as your digital fitness companions, allowing you to monitor physical activity, set exercise goals, and track progress over time. These apps can record daily steps, calories burned, and even sleep patterns, providing a comprehensive view of your physical health. With their user-friendly interfaces, they make it easy to visualize your achievements and stay motivated on your fitness journey.

When it comes to mental and emotional wellness, apps like Calm or Headspace serve as digital sanctuaries, offering guided meditation sessions that help reduce stress and promote mindfulness. These apps cater to beginners and experienced practitioners, providing a variety of courses and exercises that fit into any schedule. Whether you're seeking a moment of peace during a hectic day or establishing a regular meditation practice, these apps offer tools that cultivate a sense of inner peace and balance. Their soothing voices and tranquil music create an atmosphere conducive to restfulness, making them a delightful addition to your daily routine. By integrating these practices, you create space for reflection and rejuvenation, enhancing your overall well-being.

Choosing the right app can feel overwhelming with so many options available. Start by considering your personal health goals and the specific features you need. User-friendliness is key; look for apps with intuitive navigation that simplify your experience.

Customer reviews can also offer insights into an app's effectiveness and reliability. Pay attention to feedback from users who share similar goals or challenges as you. Additionally, explore apps that align with your lifestyle, whether you need reminders for hydration, guidance for nutrition, or tools for stress management. Prioritizing apps that offer personalized recommendations ensures that the tools you choose genuinely support your wellness journey.

Integrating these digital tools into your daily habits is an empowering step toward achieving your wellness goals. Set reminders for exercise or hydration to ensure these activities become part of your routine. Many apps offer customizable notifications that gently prompt you to move, drink water, or take a mindful break. These reminders act as nudges, keeping you on track and reinforcing positive habits. Use the tracking features to celebrate small victories, whether that's meeting a step goal or completing a meditation session. By acknowledging these achievements, you build momentum and confidence, inspiring continued progress.

To illustrate the power of these tools, contemplate creating a personalized wellness plan that incorporates various apps. Start by identifying your primary health objectives, such as improving fitness, reducing stress, or enhancing sleep quality. Then, select apps that cater to each goal, ensuring they complement one another. For instance, pair a fitness app with a nutrition tracker to gain a holistic view of your physical health. Simultaneously, integrate a meditation app to support emotional well-being. This tailored approach allows you to address multiple aspects of wellness, creating a balanced and comprehensive plan that adapts to your evolving needs.

Visual Element: App Selection Checklist

Consider using a checklist to help you choose the right apps. List your health goals and essential features you desire in an app, such as tracking capabilities, user interface, and community support. Check user reviews and ratings to gauge satisfaction. Evaluate free trials or basic versions before committing to premium options. This checklist will guide your selection and ensure you find apps that resonate with your lifestyle and aspirations.

8.3 ONLINE LEARNING PLATFORMS: EXPANDING YOUR HORIZONS

Imagine sitting comfortably at home, sipping your morning coffee, as you explore a world of knowledge available at your fingertips. This is the promise of online learning platforms like Coursera, edX, and Khan Academy. These websites offer an expansive range of courses, covering everything from ancient history to advanced computer science. Whether you're rekindling an old interest or diving into an entirely new field, these platforms provide the resources you need. Specialized platforms also cater to artistic pursuits, offering lessons in painting, music, and even creative writing, allowing you to nurture your talents and passions with expert guidance.

The beauty of online education lies in its flexibility. Unlike traditional classrooms, digital learning allows you to set your own pace. You can pause, rewind, and revisit lectures whenever you wish, making it ideal for those who learn best through repetition. This self-directed pace can relieve the pressure of strict deadlines, letting you absorb information in a manner that suits you best. Additionally, these platforms bring global universities right into your living room. Suppose you are taking a course from a prestigious institution without the need to travel. This access to diverse perspectives enriches your understanding and broadens your horizons, connecting you with a global community of learners.

When selecting courses, it's essential to choose ones that resonate with your interests and align with your skill level. Start by browsing course catalogs and reading detailed descriptions. Pay attention to prerequisites to ensure you have the foundational knowledge needed to succeed. Reviews from past students can also provide valuable insights into the course's quality and relevance. These reviews often highlight the strengths and weaknesses of the course, offering a candid look at what you can expect. By taking the time to research and select courses thoughtfully, you maximize your learning experience and ensure it is both rewarding and enjoyable.

Active engagement in online learning can significantly enhance your experience. Rather than passively consuming content, seek out opportunities to interact with fellow learners. Many platforms offer discussion forums where you can ask questions, share insights, and engage in meaningful dialogue. These forums create a sense of community, allowing you to connect with others who share your interests. Additionally, think about joining study groups, either virtually or locally, to further enrich your learning. Collaborating with others deepens your understanding and provides accountability, helping you stay committed to your educational goals.

Setting personal learning objectives is another way to make the most of your online education. Start by outlining what you hope to achieve with each course. These objectives can be specific, such as mastering a particular skill, or more general, like gaining a broader understanding of a topic. By defining clear goals, you create a roadmap for your learning journey, guiding your focus and efforts. As you progress, regularly assess your progress toward these objectives. Reflecting on your achievements and areas for improvement helps you stay motivated and ensures your learning remains purposeful and aligned with your aspirations.

Interactive Element: Course Selection Worksheet

Consider creating a course selection worksheet to help you select the right courses. List the topics you're interested in exploring and note any prerequisites you might need. Include sections for course reviews and personal objectives. Use this worksheet as a guide to evaluate potential courses, ensuring they match your interests and learning goals. This structured approach helps streamline your decision-making process, making it easier to find classes that enrich your knowledge and skills.

8.4 STAYING CONNECTED: SOCIAL MEDIA AND COMMUNICATION TOOLS

Envision sitting on your patio with a glass of lemonade, while scrolling through photos of your granddaughter's birthday party or your friend's new garden. This is the magic of social media—bringing distant loved ones closer, one post at a time. Platforms like Facebook, Twitter, and Instagram offer a virtual window into the lives of family and friends, allowing you to share life updates, photos, and videos with just a few clicks. Whether it's a snapshot of your latest project or a heartfelt message to a friend across the country, these platforms keep the lines of communication open, fostering connections regardless of distance. Social media has transformed the way we interact, creating a sense of community that defies geographical boundaries.

Beyond sharing updates, social platforms offer a wealth of opportunities to engage with diverse interests and communities. You can join groups aligned with your hobbies, such as knitting clubs, book discussions, or travel forums, where you can exchange ideas and experiences with like-minded individuals. These interactions enrich your social life and provide a sense of belonging in a broader community. Additionally, social media lets you stay informed about global events, trends, and innovations, keeping you connected to the world while nurturing personal connections. It's a dynamic space where relationships thrive, supported by the constant flow of information and interaction.

In addition to social media, communication tools like Zoom and Skype have revolutionized the way we connect face-to-face, even when miles apart. These video-calling apps transform ordinary conversations into meaningful interactions, allowing you to see the smiles and hear the laughter of loved ones in real time. Picture hosting a virtual family reunion, where relatives from different parts of the world gather on a screen, sharing stories and laughter as if sitting around the same table. These tools have become invaluable, particularly in times when physical gatherings aren't possible, ensuring that the warmth of family and friendship remains uninterrupted.

Messaging apps like WhatsApp and Signal add another layer of convenience, facilitating instant communication that feels personal and immediate. Whether it's a quick hello or an in-depth conversation, these apps keep you connected through text, voice, and even video messages. They're perfect for staying in touch with friends and family, sharing moments as they happen, or coordinating plans with ease. The simplicity and accessibility of these tools make them a staple in modern communication, bridging gaps and strengthening bonds across distances. With features like group chats and media sharing, they enrich interactions and make staying in touch effortless.

As you engage with these digital tools, it's vital to prioritize privacy and security. Adjusting your privacy settings on social media controls what you share and with whom. Take the time to explore each platform's privacy options, ensuring that only trusted individuals can view your posts and updates. Be mindful of the information you share publicly and avoid posting sensitive details like your home address or travel plans. Regularly examine your friend lists and connections, keeping your network secure and personalized. Additionally, familiarize yourself with the security features of messaging apps, such as end-to-end encryption, which protects your conversations from unauthorized access.

To further safeguard your online interactions, stay informed about the potential risks associated with digital communication. Be cautious about accepting friend requests from unknown individuals and avoid clicking on suspicious links, which could lead to phishing attempts or malware. Educate yourself on recognizing scams and fraudulent events to ensure that your digital presence remains safe and secure. By staying vigilant and informed, you can enjoy the benefits of social media and communication tools while maintaining control over your online privacy.

8.5 SMART HOMES AND TECH GADGETS: CREATING A CONVENIENT LIFESTYLE

Picture this: you're sitting in your favorite armchair and with a simple voice command, the room adjusts to the perfect temperature, your favorite playlist starts, and the lights dim to a cozy hue. This scenario isn't just a vision of the future; it's the reality of smart home technology today. Smart devices like thermostats and security cameras have revolutionized our living spaces, turning them into personalized havens that cater to our needs. These devices enhance convenience and bolster safety, offering peace of mind with features like remote monitoring and alerts. Think of a smart thermostat that learns your schedule, automatically adjusting to save energy and maintain comfort. Or a security camera that keeps an eye on your home, sending notifications directly to your smartphone whenever motion is detected.

Voice-activated assistants, such as Amazon Alexa or Google Home, add another layer of ease to daily life. These devices serve as personal assistants, capable of managing everything from setting reminders to ordering groceries. Imagine waking up in the morning and asking your assistant about the weather forecast, your schedule for the day, or even a new recipe to try for dinner. With simple voice commands, you can control various smart devices throughout your home, streamlining tasks that once required multiple steps. The beauty of these assistants lies in their ability to integrate with a wide array of smart gadgets, creating a seamless ecosystem that responds to your voice.

Installing smart home technology might seem daunting, but the process is often smoother than anticipated. Begin with the basics, like setting up a smart thermostat. These devices typically come with user-friendly apps that guide you through installation. Secure the thermostat to the wall, connect it to your Wi-Fi network, and configure it through the app. Similarly, security cameras often involve mounting the camera, connecting it to a power source, and syncing it with an app for live monitoring. Voice-activated assistants usually require plugging into a power outlet, connecting to Wi-Fi, and completing a quick setup through a smartphone app. Once integrated, these devices can be customized to fit your lifestyle, ensuring they meet your preferences and needs.

As you explore smart home technology, keep an open mind to the myriads of gadgets available. Wearable tech, like smartwatches, provides valuable insights into health, tracking steps, heart rate, and even sleep patterns. These devices serve as personal health monitors, encouraging you to stay active and informed about your well-being. Consider the convenience of receiving notifications, calls, and messages right on your wrist, allowing you to stay connected without constantly checking your phone. The integration of health apps and smartwatches creates a comprehensive wellness toolkit that supports your lifestyle.

Curiosity and willingness to experiment with new technology can transform your home into a space that anticipates your needs. Whether it's automated lighting that adjusts based on the time of day or a smart fridge that suggests recipes based on its contents, these innovations simplify daily tasks and enhance quality of life. As you become more familiar with smart technology, you'll discover endless possibilities for customization, allowing each device to serve a purpose tailored to your routine. With each addition, your home becomes a more intuitive environment, fostering comfort and efficiency.

8.6 CYBERSECURITY: PROTECTING YOUR DIGITAL PRESENCE

In our increasingly digital lives, protecting personal information online has become crucial. While a gateway to convenience and connection, the internet can also be risky if not navigated with caution. Identity theft and data breaches are not just abstract threats; they can have real, tangible impacts on your life. Visualize logging into your bank account only to find your funds mysteriously depleted or receiving bills for purchases you never made. These scenarios, unfortunately, are realities for many who fall victim to online scams. It's important to understand that cyber-criminals often target those they perceive as vulnerable, hoping to exploit any gaps in security. Therefore, taking proactive measures to secure your digital presence is not only wise but necessary.

Creating strong, unique passwords for all your accounts is one of the simplest yet most effective strategies to enhance your online safety. Think of your password as the key to your digital home. Would you leave your front door unlocked? Similarly, a weak pass-word is an open invitation to cyber intruders. Use a mix of letters, numbers, and special characters to make your passwords as complex as possible. Avoid using easily guessed information like birthdays or common words. Give thought to using a password manager to keep track of your passwords securely. These tools generate and store complex passwords, so you don't have to remember each one. In addition to strong passwords, enabling two-factor authentication adds an extra layer of security. This method requires a second form of verification, such as a text message code, before granting access to your account. It's like having a deadbolt on your digital door.

Recognizing and avoiding online scams is another critical aspect of cybersecurity. Scammers are clever, often disguising their attacks to look legitimate. Be wary of emails or messages from unknown sources that request personal information or urge immediate action. Common red flags include poor grammar, urgent language, and unfamiliar email addresses. Phishing scams often mimic trusted institutions, like your bank, to trick you into revealing sensitive information. Always verify the sender's authenticity before clicking on any links or downloading attach-ments. When in doubt, contact the company directly using contact information from their official website. Staying informed about these tactics can empower you to recognize and avoid potential threats.

Regular updates and security practices are your best defense against cyber threats. Much like a car needs regular maintenance, your devices and software require updates to run smoothly and securely. Software updates often include patches for security vulnerabilities that, if left unaddressed, could be exploited by hackers. Set your devices to update automatically, ensuring you always have the latest protections in place. Installing reputable antivirus software is another vital practice, as it detects and neutralizes malicious software that may try to infiltrate your system. These programs run quietly in the background, offering peace of mind as you navigate the digital world. Regularly scanning your devices can catch potential threats early, preventing them from causing harm.

Textual Element: Cybersecurity Checklist

Examine using a cybersecurity checklist to bolster your digital defenses. This tool can guide you through essential steps, such as reviewing and updating your passwords, checking for software updates, and ensuring your antivirus protection is current. It also includes reminders to enable two-factor authentication and verify the authenticity of emails before responding. This checklist serves as a practical resource to reinforce your cybersecurity routine, keeping your digital presence secure and your mind at ease.

Protecting your digital footprint gives you the confidence to explore the internet's vast opportunities without fear. As you continue to engage with technology, these practices will become second nature, allowing you to focus on the digital world's positive aspects. With cybersecurity as your foundation, you are well-prepared to navigate the digital landscape safely and securely, ensuring your online interactions remain positive and productive.

PASSING THE TORCH

Now that you've explored how to redefine retirement on your own terms—finding purpose, nurturing relationships, and embracing this new chapter with confidence—it's time to pay it forward.

By sharing your honest opinion of this book on Amazon, you'll guide other women to the support and inspiration they're searching for. Your review can shine a light for someone who's just beginning their journey and help her discover how to create a fulfilling retirement that's uniquely hers.

Thank you for being part of this empowering journey. Retirement is redefined when we share what we've learned—and you're helping me inspire women everywhere to approach this chapter with excitement and possibility.

Scan the QR code to leave your review on Amazon.

With appreciation,

Victoria Spring

CONCLUSION

As we close the pages of this book, I invite you to pause and reflect on our journey together. Throughout these chapters, we've explored the myriad facets of retirement, uncovering the secrets to a joyful and engaged lifestyle. We've delved into the importance of redefining your identity, achieving financial peace, nurturing social connections, and embracing the possibilities that this new chapter brings. Each insight has been a steppingstone, guiding you towards a retirement that is as unique and vibrant as you are.

The path to a fulfilling retirement is paved with self-discovery and growth. As you embark on this adventure, remember that you hold the power to shape your experience. Accept the opportunity to explore new passions, whether it's diving into a fascinating subject through online learning or unleashing your creativity through a long-forgotten hobby. These pursuits enrich your mind and foster a sense of purpose and vitality.

Financial security is the basis of a carefree retirement. By implementing the strategies discussed, such as smart budgeting and savvy investment choices, you can build a solid foundation for enjoying your golden years with peace of mind. Remember, wealth isn't just about numbers in a bank account; it's about the freedom to live life on your terms without the burden of financial stress.

The relationships you nurture during retirement create a network of love and support. Strengthen bonds with family and form new friendships through shared interests. In life's challenges, these connections become a sanctuary of strength, laughter, and comfort. Embrace the sense of belonging that comes from community, knowing you are never alone on this journey.

As you craft your daily routines, prioritize activities that bring you joy and fulfillment. Infuse your days with purpose, whether it's through volunteering, pursuing a long-held passion, or simply savoring the beauty of a quiet moment. Remember, retirement is not about filling time; it's about living each day to its fullest, on your own terms.

Throughout this book, we've explored a myriad of ways technology can enhance your retirement experience. From staying connected with loved ones across the miles to unlocking new worlds of knowledge, these digital tools are your allies. Support the opportunities they provide, while always prioritizing your well-being and security in the online space.

As you navigate the challenges and triumphs of retirement, remember that you are the author of your own story. Each day presents a new page, waiting to be filled with the adventures, laughter, and love that you choose. Espouse the power of self-reflection, taking moments to assess your journey and adjust your course as needed. This is your time to dream big, to chase the passions that set your soul on fire, and to create a retirement that exceeds your wildest expectations.

I encourage you to take the insights and strategies from this book and weave them into the fabric of your life. Start small, implementing one change at a time, and watch as your retirement blossoms into a masterpiece of your own making. Seek out the company of other women who share your aspirations, joining online communities or local groups where you can exchange ideas, offer support, and celebrate each other's successes.

So, my dear reader, go forth with confidence and joy. The world is waiting for the unique gifts that only you can bring. Embrace this new chapter with a heart full of hope and a spirit ready for adventure. Your retirement is a story waiting to be written, and I can't wait to see the masterpiece you create.

Nurture the relationships that matter most, whether it's strengthening bonds with family or building new friendships through shared interests. In the face of life's challenges, these connections serve as a source of strength, laughter, and comfort. Champion the power of community, knowing that you are never alone on this journey.

Above all, remember that you are not alone in this journey. As you turn the final page of this book, know that I am here, cheering you on every step of the way. Your retirement is a canvas, waiting to be painted with the vibrant hues of your dreams and desires. Embrace this opportunity with open arms, knowing that the best is yet to come.

REFERENCES

Regions. (n.d.). *Rethinking retirement: 3 women share their stories*. Retrieved from https://www.regions.com/insights/personal/retirement/establishing-a-plan/rethinking-retirement-3-women-share-their-stories

Conservatory Senior Living. (n.d.). *Personal development tips for seniors*. Retrieved from https://www.conservatoryseniorliving.com/senior-living-blog/personal-development-tips-for-seniors/

Yale School of Public Health. (n.d.). *Early retirement impacts mental health of blue-collar women more than white-collar peers*. Retrieved from https://ysph.yale.edu/news-article/retirement-impacts-mental-health-of-blue-collar-women-more-than-white-collar-peers/

Women's Institute for a Secure Retirement. (n.d.). *National Resource Center on Women and Retirement*. Retrieved from https://wiserwomen.org/national-resource-center-on-women-and-retirement-2/

SeniorLiving.org. (n.d.). *The best budgeting apps for seniors*. Retrieved from https://www.seniorliving.org/finance/budgeting-apps/

National Council on Aging. (n.d.). *How can I boost my Social Security benefit?*. Retrieved from https://www.ncoa.org/article/get-more-money-from-social-security-7-tips-to-max-out-your-benefits/

NerdWallet. (n.d.). *Best brokers for beginner investors: Top picks for 2025*. Retrieved from https://www.nerdwallet.com/best/investing/online-brokers-for-beginners

AARP. (n.d.). *15 part-time jobs for retirees (no degree required!)*. Retrieved from https://www.aarp.org/work/job-search/retiree-part-time-jobs/

Senior Helpers. (2023, April 10). *The benefits of joining a senior center or club*. Retrieved from https://www.seniorhelpers.com/or/corvallis/resources/blogs/2023-04-10/

Sonida Senior Living. (n.d.). *The best social media sites for seniors: A guide to staying connected and engaged*. Retrieved from https://www.sonidaseniorliving.com/the-best-social-media-sites-for-seniors-a-guide-to-staying-connected-and-engaged/

Ocean of Solitude. (n.d.). *How technology is redefining long-distance friendships*. Retrieved from https://oceanofsolitude.com/how-technology-is-redefining-long-distance-friendships/

AmeriCorps. (n.d.). *AmeriCorps Seniors*. Retrieved from https://americorps.gov/serve/americorps-seniors

Stellar Living. (n.d.). *How to create a masterful morning routine for seniors*. Retrieved from https://stellarliving.com/create-a-masterful-morning-routine/

Kiplinger. (n.d.). *9 tips for better time management in retirement*. Retrieved from https://www.kiplinger.com/retirement/601545/9-tips-for-better-time-management-in-retirement

Senior Lifestyle. (n.d.). *Why lifelong learning is important for seniors*. Retrieved from https://www.seniorlifestyle.com/resources/blog/lifelong-learning-for-seniors/

Upscoop. (n.d.). *Evening reflection: The key to personal growth and success*. Retrieved from https://www.upscoop.com/evening-reflection-the-key-to-personal-growth-and-success

Road Scholar. (n.d.). *Best retirement hobbies: Ideas for seniors over 60*. Retrieved from https://www.roadscholar.org/blog/12-best-retirement-hobbies/

Harvard Business Review. (2017, February). *Lifelong learning is good for your health, your wallet, and your social life*. Retrieved from https://hbr.org/2017/02/lifelong-learning-is-good-for-your-health-your-wallet-and-your-social-life

Independent Financial Services. (n.d.). *Encore careers: A new chapter for women in retirement*. Retrieved from https://www.ifstampabay.com/encore-careers-a-new-chapter-for-women-in-retirement/

VolunteerMatch. (n.d.). *VolunteerMatch - Where volunteering begins*. Retrieved from https://www.volunteermatch.org/

Verywell Mind. (n.d.). *How to set boundaries with your adult children*. Retrieved from https://www.verywellmind.com/setting-boundaries-with-adult-children-8686106

Marriage.com. (n.d.). *8 considerate ways to strengthen your marriage in retirement*. Retrieved from https://www.marriage.com/advice/marriage-fitness/strengthen-your-marriage-in-retirement/

Greater Good Science Center. (n.d.). *How to navigate the joys and challenges of grandparenting*. Retrieved from https://greatergood.berkeley.edu/article/item/how_to_navigate_the_joys_and_challenges_of_grandparenting

Mental Health America. (n.d.). *Caregiving and the sandwich generation*. Retrieved from https://mhanational.org/caregiving-and-sandwich-generation

Senior Lifestyle. (n.d.). *7 best exercises for seniors (and a few to avoid!)*. Retrieved from https://www.seniorlifestyle.com/resources/blog/7-best-exercises-for-seniors-and-a-few-to-avoid/

MedlinePlus. (n.d.). *Nutrition for older adults*. Retrieved from https://medlineplus.gov/nutritionforolderadults.html

Wirecutter. (2025). *The 4 best meditation apps of 2025*. Retrieved from https://www.nytimes.com/wirecutter/reviews/best-meditation-apps/

National Institute on Aging. (n.d.). *Cognitive health and older adults*. Retrieved from https://www.nia.nih.gov/health/brain-health/cognitive-health-and-older-adults

Cyber-Seniors. (n.d.). *Cyber-Seniors*. Retrieved from https://cyberseniors.org/

Byvi. (2023, October 5). *Top health apps for women to master a wellness journey*. Retrieved from https://byvi.co/2023/10/05/health-apps-for-women/

Senior Planet from AARP. (n.d.). *Online classes for seniors*. Retrieved from https://seniorplanet.org/classes/

Cybersecurity and Infrastructure Security Agency. (n.d.). *Cybersecurity and older Americans*. Retrieved from https://www.cisa.gov/sites/default/files/publications/Cybersecurity%2520and%2520Older%2520Americans.pdf